the economics of development: problems and policies

Reading economics
Editor: Geoffrey Denton, Reader in Economics in the University of Reading

the economics of development: problems and policies
Mathew McQueen

Weidenfeld & Nicolson
London

ISBN 0 297 76534 5 cased
ISBN 0 297 76535 3 paperback
Printed by Redwood Press Limited
Trowbridge, Wiltshire

contents

author's preface

Anyone teaching a course in development economics is immediately faced with a dilemma. Most students will have very little knowledge of the economic and social conditions of developing countries; at the same time they naturally wish to come to grips immediately with the problems and policy issues facing these countries. In addition, students can only be expected to have a basic knowledge of economic theory and little practice in the application of this knowledge.

Despite this, introductory courses in development economics are clearly justified, not only to meet the strong interest of students in the problems of the developing countries, but also as part of the general education of economists. Economics is fundamentally concerned with the improvement of the material conditions of mankind. It would therefore appear decidedly unbalanced for economists to emerge from their studies full of ideas for raising the already high standards of living of the minority of developed countries, and totally ignorant of the economic conditions facing two thirds of the world! In applying their knowledge of economic theory to the very different economic and institutional conditions of the developing countries, students also learn to question the implicit assumptions upon which traditional theory is based.

This book aims to meet these requirements by providing the minimum factual knowledge and theoretical basis for examining major policy issues. The policy issues in turn have been selected on the basis of their current importance and their susceptibility to examination, using the basic tools of economic analysis. Emphasis has been placed on the way in which tools of analysis, originally designed for developed countries, have had to be modified to take account of the wide differences in economic and social conditions of the developing countries. The aim is to provide an overall view of some of the most important problems and policy issues concerning the developing countries, briefly summarising some of the most important theoretical and empirical writings in the field. The reader can then select those issues which particularly interest him and study them in more detail by using the references listed at the end of the chapters.

In the course of writing this book I have benefited considerably from the advice and encouragement of my colleagues at the University of Reading. In particular I would like to express my gratitude to a former colleague, Professor Manfred Streit of the University of Mannheim and to the editor, Geoffrey Denton, who read through the whole book and made many invaluable comments; to Professor Geoffrey Maynard for his advice, encouragement and extremely useful comments; to Professor John Dunning and Robert Pearce for permission to use some of their unpublished work on private overseas investment in developing countries, and to Graham Bird, Mark Casson and Robert Pearce for their unfailing help in answering numerous queries and directing me to important publications. Martin Kebbell, as a student, assisted in the preparation of the statistics.

Errors that remain are of course entirely my own responsibility, particularly since those who kindly agreed to comment on the book were invariably asked to do so in a very short period of time.

Finally, I would like to express my thanks to the students, who over the past few years have cheerfully submitted themselves to my experiments in teaching development economics.

M. Mc Queen
Reading, September 1971.

chapter 1

the developing countries: a description

1.1 Introduction

Anyone first approaching the subject may be confused by the multitude of terms describing this area of study, ranging from the older ones of *underdeveloped* and *poor countries* to the more modern ones of *the third world, developing,* and *less developed* countries (LDCs). Although essentially interchangeable the choice of terms reflects how optimistic you happen to be about the future prospects of these countries, the political sensitivity of the subject and the need for writers to avoid repetition and to differentiate their product.

This proliferation of names also reflects the lack of a clear and unambiguous criterion for selecting these countries. What does it matter whether we have an unambiguous and quantifiable definition of development? Surely we all can recognise which are the underdeveloped countries and which are not? To a large extent this is true although doubts may begin to appear when considering whether countries like Israel or Argentina can be grouped as underdeveloped along with countries like Burma and India.

Fundamentally, progress in understanding the process of development depends on ability to compare one state of development with another, and on attempts to isolate those factors which have caused these changes. After building up knowledge in this way it is possible to construct theories which will be valid in a fairly wide range of circumstances. The chain of reasoning can begin equally, of course, with the theories which are then tested. In either case we are lost if we cannot say which situation is more or less developed than another.

At a more practical level the state of development of a country is one of the criteria, though not necessarily the most important, used by aid giving agencies.[1] Similarly the rate of development is often used as a measure of the efficiency with which this aid has been applied.

In drawing up a development strategy, governments often take a close look at countries which have broadly similar resource endowments to their own but have achieved a higher level of development. By such comparisons they hope to acquire

1 For example at the third United Nations Conference on Trade and Development in 1972, the developed countries agreed to resolutions requiring them to give special assistance to the least developed countries with incomes per head of less than $100.

ideas on useful development policies and also some indicators of the likely pattern of future output and expenditure.

1.2 International comparisons using economic statistics

The most widely used measure is that of per capita Gross National Product using United States dollars as the common denominator. There are enormous difficulties involved in the use of this measure. In particular, no welfare conclusions can be drawn from these figures without a whole series of value judgements immediately becoming involved. However even taking the point of view that the exercise is limited to making a rough approximation of the resources available to these countries, an enormous gap is revealed between 'rich' and 'poor' countries. For example the income difference between the United States and India appears to be in the ratio of 45:1, and between the United Kingdom and India, 22:1. The value of GNP in developing countries is probably considerably underestimated by this measure, but even multiplying India's per capita GNP in dollars by a factor of three still produces a very low relative level of income per head.

It may also be argued that the concept of the 'average' level of income is particularly misleading because the distribution of income is usually much more unequal in the less developed than in the developed countries. Allowing for this the original ratios are possibly closer to the real difference for the majority of people in these countries.

Whatever qualifications we make, the gap between rich and poor countries is clearly enormous. It is usual to take a figure of $500 as a conservative dividing line between developed and less developed countries and add some 'intermediate' countries, mostly in southern Europe, with rather higher income levels. On this definition the Pearson report reached the broad conclusion that the 'third world' comprises nearly 70 per cent of the world's population but has only 12 per cent of the world's income. The gap can only be reduced by the less developed countries sustaining a higher rate of growth of output per head than the developed countries.

The rate of growth of output of the LDCs over the postwar period has certainly been encouraging. In the period 1950-70 the annual rate of growth of GDP of the developing countries was just over 5 per cent, accelerating to nearly 6 per cent in 1965-70. This average of course conceals considerable variations. But especially in the last decade the majority of developing countries have recorded quite high rates of growth, far removed from the picture of general stagnation and also, on average, in excess of the 5 per cent average annual growth of output in the developed countries. Of course to reduce the gap in income levels appreciably, in a reasonable period of time, the LDCs must record much higher rates of growth since they are developing from a much smaller base.

Table 1
Ranking of less-developed countries[1] by average annual per cent changes
in real product per capita 1960 - 1970

countries with an annual average per capita growth rate of over 5%	per capita GNP 1969 $	total real product	per capita real product
Libya	1,510	21·6	17·3
Taiwan	300	9·9	6·9
Greece	840	7·4	6·7
SPAIN	820	7·6	6·6
SOUTH KOREA	210	9·3	6·5
Iran	350	8·8	5·7
Yugoslavia	580	6·8	5·6
Ivory Coast	240	7·8	5·4
Israel	1,570	8·5	5·1
Cyprus	830	6·2	5·1
3·5% to 5%			
THAILAND	160	8·0	4·8
Panama	660	8·1	4·7
MEXICO	580	7·2	3·6

countries with an annual average per capita growth rate of: 2% to 3·5%	per capita GNP 1969 $	total real product	per capita real product
Angola	–	4·4	3·1
Nicaragua	380	6·6	3·0
Costa Rica	510	6·2	3·0
Malaysia	340	6·0	3·0
Mozambique	210	4·2	2·9
Bolivia	160	5·5	2·8
TURKEY	350	5·4	2·8
BRAZIL	270	5·6	2·7
Argentina	1,060	4·2	2·6
PAKISTAN	110	5·3	2·5
Ethiopia	–	4·6	2·5
El Salvador	390	5·8	2·4
Jamaica	550	4·5	2·4
PHILLIPPINES	210	5·7	2·3
UNITED ARAB REPUBLIC	160	4·8	2·2
Venezuela	1,000	5·7	2·1
Guatemala	350	5·2	2·1
Tunisia	230	4·3	2·1
Kenya	130	5·0	2·0
Ceylon	190	4·4	2·0

Table 1 (cont'd.)

countries with an annual average per capita growth rate of: less than 2%	per capita GNP 1969 $	total real product	per capita real product
Colombia	290	5·2	1·9
Chile	510	4·3	1·9
Uganda	110	4·4	1·9
Tanzania	80	4·3	1·8
Zambia	290	4·9	1·8
–	–	–	–
Congo (Kinshasa)	90	2·2	1·7
Ecuador	220	5·1	1·6
Peru	330	4·7	1·6
INDIA	110	3·7	1·5
Paraguay	240	4·4	1·3
Sudan	110	4·1	1·3
Morocco	190	3·8	0·9
Dominican Republic	280	3·7	0·1
Ghana	190	2·6	0
NIGERIA	220	2·3	0
Uruguay	560	1·1	−0·2

1 The countries included in the table represent 86 per cent of total population of less-developed countries, of which the countries shown in capital letters account for nearly 70 per cent. Source OECD Development Centre

Source [1] OECD Devlopment Assistance Committee 'Review' 1970

[2] Per Capita GNP World Bank 1972

However the situation only becomes alarming in respect of *per capita* rates, which present an entirely different picture, shown in table 1. The annual growth of population in the developed world has been just over one per cent but in the developing countries the average has been 2·5 per cent and shows every indication of being higher in future years. In terms of per capita income therefore the gap between rich and poor countries is widening. It is easy to conclude from this that the economic case for population limitation is obvious. However the issue is not so clear cut since a number of economists argue that rapid growth of population can be expected to accelerate the growth of output. Thus a reduction in the growth of population could cause economic stagnation. This argument will be examined in chapter 2, leading to the conclusion that in fact there is a strong presumption that reducing the rate of growth of population will accelerate the growth of output even in the low density lands of tropical Africa.

Many problems of interpretation of the per capita GNP measure result from the conversion of this indicator, originally expressed in national currencies, to United States dollars. At best the exchange rate only equates the relative prices of internationally traded goods and services. It does not reflect the prices of the mass of goods and services produced and consumed within the developing countries which do not enter into trade with the United States. In addition exchange rates are of course 'managed' and are not necessarily equilibrium rates even for items entering into international trade.

Various attempts have been made to correct exchange rates for differences in purchasing power between countries of similar income levels and consumption patterns by drawing up a common 'basket of goods' with weights attached, to express the importance of these goods in total consumption. In addition, corrections are made to prices for differences in the quality of the goods. A pioneering and still unsurpassed study is that by Gilbert and Kravis. This brief look at the restrictive conditions which have to be fulfilled in order to produce accurate purchasing power parities indicates the impossibility of performing such an exercise as between developed and less developed countries. Income levels, consumption patterns, tastes, market conditions, quality of goods and so on are vastly different: therefore between a developed and an underdeveloped country there will be two quite different sets of prices at which to value the output of the two countries. The national output of India can be measured either at US prices or at Indian prices, and similarly for US national output. In either case the result would not mean very much. It is therefore better to confine comparisons of real income levels to countries with broadly similar income levels, tastes, etc.

National accounts can still be used however, avoiding the pitfalls of using values, by dealing instead in proportions. It has long been argued, notably by Clark (1940) and Kuznets, that the level of development of a country can be identified according to the proportion of output derived from primary (agriculture and extractive industries), secondary (manufacturing, processing etc.) and tertiary (services) activities. The less developed a country, the greater the proportion of its total output which is derived from primary production simply because this is the structure of demand at low levels of income. As incomes rise and the economy becomes more developed, so the pattern of demand shifts to manufactured and processed goods and this is reflected in the composition of total output. Of course, this generalisation is open to a number of objections, for example that it ignores the fact that a country may have a relatively large agricultural sector simply because it has a comparative advantage in agricultural products and not because it has a low level of income per head. Despite these obvious objections there does appear to be considerable empirical justification for the general concept that as countries become more developed so the importance of the agricultural sector declines and the share of industry in national output rises. Chenery for example found that the share of industrial output in the national product rose from 17 per cent at an income level of $100 to 38 per cent at a level of $1,000, while primary production declined from 45 per cent to 15 per cent, with very few countries showing wide deviations from this pattern. This feature of the development process is illustrated in table 2 where it can be seen that the agricultural sector in developing countries typically accounts for 30 to 50 per cent of GDP, in contrast to three per cent in the UK and US, and 11 per cent in France. Over the period 1953-68 there has been a tendency in developing countries for the importance of agriculture to decline and for the share of industry in national output to rise to between 10 and 25 per cent, and in the semi-developed case of Argentina to 36 per cent. But with few exceptions the shift in shares has not been large despite quite high rates of growth of manufacturing output. For example in the period 1960-68 Pakistan recorded an average annual growth of manufacturing output of 11 per cent but, given the relatively small size of the industrial sector in total output, this meant only a small increase in its share of national output. So long as the agricultural sector comprises the largest share of domestic product, then the rate of growth of the economy must fundamentally depend on the fortunes of agriculture. The share of agriculture in GDP, while significant, under-estimates its importance in determining standards of living. Thus in Brazil agriculture produces 30 per cent of the domestic product but provides employment for 50 per cent of the total labour force. Even more striking are the examples of Kenya and Thailand where agriculture produces 30 to 35 per cent of total output and employs at least 80 per cent of the labour force. Given that the majority of the population live in and depend on the agricultural sector it follows that most of the impact of the growth of population will be felt in this sector. Policy must therefore be directed towards raising the ability of agriculture to absorb the increase in numbers until the pressure is relieved by the increase in size of the manufacturing sector. In chapter Three one of the dangers of the 'green revolution', (ie new high yield varieties of seeds combined with a 'package' of fertilisers, water etc) is discussed showing that it may result in spectacular increases in output at considerable social cost, though this need not happen provided appropriate policies are pursued.

Another characteristic of a number of developing countries is the concentration of their exports into food and raw materials. For developing countries as a whole in the period 1965-7 just under 50 per cent of their total export earnings, including fuels, came from these two categories. The dependence on food and raw material exports varies considerably between countries. For instance for Argentina, Brazil, Thailand, Ghana, Uganda and the Phillipines some 80 to 90 per cent of their exports come from the agricultural sector alone, (see table 9). In addition there is often a heavy dependence on a particular commodity; such as Ghana and Nigeria on cocoa, Colombia on coffee,

Table 2
The structure of production in 1953 and 1968, in selected developed and less developed countries

	industry as % of GDP		agriculture as % of GDP	
	1953	1968	1953	1968
Australia	32	34	14	10
New Zealand	24	27	24	17
UK	40	39	5	3
US	35	32	5	3
Canada	35	32	11	6
France	41	41	12	11
W. Germany	46	43	9	5
Japan	26	29	21	12
Italy	31	32	23	12
Spain	31	31	22	16
Portugal	27	37	32	20
Morocco	18	23	34	30
Algeria	19	22	30	16
Tunisia	16	22	25	16
UAR	na	23	32	28
Kenya	10	14	47	35
Nigeria	5	13	65	56
Zambia	na	23	na	28
Jamaica	17	26	21	11
Argentina	28	36	20	15
Brazil	24	29	29	30
Colombia	18	21	38	31
Burma	7	10	34	34
Ceylon	5	9	54	40
India	17	15	51	52
Pakistan	8	12	53	47
Phillipines	18	20	34	33
Thailand	13	16	43	31
Taiwan	37	24	37	24

Source UN Yearbook of National Accounts Statistics

Chile and Zambia on copper. Chapter 5 shows how this concentration on primary commodities may give rise to slow growth and instability in export earnings with consequent disruption of the development effort. It would be a mistake however to regard all developing countries as producing primary commodities for export. For example India, Pakistan, Taiwan and Korea obtain 45 to 60 per cent of their export earnings from manufactures.

1.3 Social measures of development

National accounts and international trade statistics only reveal part of the overall picture of a developing country. With regard to general standards of living, 'social' statistics of health and education provide an additional insight into conditions in developing countries.

To the interested non-specialist in the developed countries one of the sharpest mental impressions of the third world may be of fairly widespread starvation and malnutrition. For the most part this impression has been conveyed by the repeated statements of the UN Food and Agricultural Organisation (FAO). Probably the most pervasive statement has been that of the FAO's first director, Lord Boyd-Orr in the early 1950s, that two-thirds of the world were starving. Colin Clark (1964) has rightly attacked such gross exaggerations and put forward his own estimates showing that starvation should be the exception. The FAO has now revised its estimates of calorie deficiency down to 10 to 15 per cent, and emphasis in recent FAO publications has instead stressed the prevalence of malnutrition, an inadequate balance of diet, which results in deficiency diseases and generally low resistance to infection. For example the Director of Statistics of the FAO has estimated that one third of the world's population suffers from protein deficiency. The FAO also publish statistics of per capita consumption of eggs, dairy products, meat, and fish, and contrast levels of consumption of these items in developed and less developed countries. Leaving aside the question of exactly how much faith can be placed in such figures there is the conceptual problem that no one can define with anything approaching accuracy, which is just how much the body needs both to stay alive and to work efficiently. This problem is further discussed in chapter 3. Global statistics are of limited value in this issue. Generally speaking the developing countries are, and in the foreseeable future will be, able to obtain sufficient food. The real problem is that of the distribution of food supplies, both throughout the year and between surplus and deficit areas within the country. Stated in this way the problem of food supplies becomes an internal one of adequate marketing, storage and transport facilities within the developing countries. Indirect evidence of improvements in food supplies is provided by the ability of developing countries to sustain dramatic increases in their populations since 1945. Fundamentally this growth of population has been the result of public health measures, imported from the developed countries and causing large decreases in mortality. The most dramatic improvement has been in infant mortality rates. For example, in India in 1945-9, the infant mortality rate was probably about 140 per thousand live births. By 1965-6 this figure had halved to 73 per thousand. Similar dramatic improvements have been recorded in practically all developing countries. The increase in overall life expectancy has not been quite so dramatic but is still substantial. So far as can be deduced from very imperfect data, life expectancy at birth is probably between 55 and 60 years in most of Latin America, and rather less in tropical Africa, probably between 35 and 45 years. Given a very slow decline in birth rates over the post-war period the net result of these changes in vital statistics has been an appreciable acceleration in the rate of growth of population. The dramatic increase in the chances of survival of children also produces a characteristically broad-based population pyramid in developing countries. The dynamics of population growth and its economic implications are more fully discussed in chapter 2. For the moment it is sufficient to have some idea of the order of magnitude of these changes and to bear in mind that although infant mortality rates have fallen considerably rates of between 40 and 70 per 1,000 live births are still quite common. The comparison with the rate of 19 in Britain provides some indication of the possibilities and implications of further improvement.

However health conditions in LDCs are far from being as good as in the developed countries. The statistics for the number of people per doctor provide a measure of standards of medical care. Usually this ranges from 2,500 to 4,000 persons per doctor, with a particularly favourable ratio of 1,400 in the Phillipines and a particularly bad proportion of 30,000 per doctor in Indonesia. These figures may be contrasted with an estimate of 600 to 800 people per doctor in developed countries. Considerable as this difference is it appreciably underestimates the situation. While 50 to 80 per cent of the population in underdeveloped countries live in rural areas, invariably 80 per cent of the doctors live and work in the towns.

It is usually considered that education, at least at an elementary level, is an important source of growth. Certainly education is an important consumption good in that it widens the experience open to individuals. From this point of view we see a particularly wide gap between rich and poor countries. For example in the UK only one per cent of the population over the age of 15 are illiterate. In a large part of Asia and Africa the proportion would be of the order of 70 per cent. Even in countries like the Phillipines which have had large injections of US aid the proportion is still about 20 per cent.

From an economic point of view however the case for mass education is not so clear cut. Resources which are used for education could be used in directly productive projects. Indeed as with expenditure on health demands are almost limitless and strict priorities must be set. In this context many economists favour investment in vocational and technical training to meet the widespread shortage of all forms of skilled labour in developing countries, and criticise the emphasis, inherited from colonial periods, on secondary and higher education in non-vocational subjects. More controversially some economists also advocate fairly long term rather than short term target dates for universal primary education, arguing that many underdeveloped economies have only a limited ability to absorb even moderately literate and numerate people. If the supply of people with primary education exceeds the demand the result will not only be a waste of resources but a dangerous build-up of frustration. A slightly different argument refers to the *content* of primary school education. This is invariably modelled on that in developed countries, and tends to produce young people intent on becoming 'clerks' and despising work on the farms and small-holdings. There is certainly considerable force behind these arguments but it is also possible to argue that advance in the agricultural sector through the spread of new techniques will depend on the receptiveness of farmers to new ideas, and that this in turn will be considerably improved by suitable elementary education.

We can now begin to form a broad picture of developing countries; a picture of low levels of per capita income; an unequal distribution of income; high rates of growth of population; a young age structure of population; considerable dependence on agriculture, especially for employment; a marked dependence on primary product exports; and so on.

But this overall picture needs much qualification. In terms of per capita income the gap between rich and poor countries appears to be widening. However in terms of health measures such as infant mortality rates and life expectancy, which must be reasonably good indicators of standards of living, the gap between rich and poor nations has narrowed very considerably in the post-war period. There is also considerable diversity within this broad picture of developing countries. For instance the per capita GNP of India, Burma, Indonesia and Nigeria is about one seventh that of Argentina, Chile and Uruguay, and one third that of Taiwan, the Phillipines, Colombia and Zambia. Dependence on agriculture and primary product exports vary considerably. Statistics also conceal a lot of information relevant to assessing standards of living. For example, Latin American countries may have much higher levels of per capita income than countries in tropical Africa but the general standard of housing is probably lower. The image of developing countries also tends to be dominated by impressions of India, with a population of over 500 million. But it is important to remember that of the one hundred or so countries which can be called underdeveloped almost three quarters have populations of less than 15 million. The average size of population in these 70 countries is five million.

1.4 Composite indicators of development

In view of this considerable diversity between countries, and the consequent inadequacy of any single measure of development, various composite measures have been put forward. The basic principle of these measures is to combine a number of economic, social and cultural factors in order to produce an overall picture of a country. One of the most impressive of these was produced by UNESCO in 1963 for Latin America. Economic variables such as per capita income, and consumption of cement, electricity, newsprint and calories, were combined with social indicators such as the proportion of urban population, the proportion of the working population employed in the primary sector, and with cultural indicators such as newspaper circulation, the proportion of the population at various levels of education, and so on. These broad measures certainly provide a more detailed picture of a particular economy but they do not help much in the fundamental problem of comparing countries' standards of living or development. If low levels of per capita income were clearly correlated with low per capita consumption of energy, cement, calories, small proportions living in towns, and so on, then countries could be ranked on this basis. But in this case any one of the measures will be as good an indicator as any other. If on the other hand some countries have low levels of per capita income but a large proportion receiving education, while others have relatively high income levels but high mortality rates, the basic difficulty remains; how to combine the measures by giving 'weights' to the various indicators, and yet avoid making value judgements, such as whether levels of calorie consumption are less important than infant mortality rates but more important than levels of illiteracy.

An important advance in producing a measure of economic welfare as distinct from total welfare has been suggested by Bacon and Beckerman. Fundamentally only income as measured in national accounts can be given a value free meaning in the sense that an increase in real domestic product can be interpreted as an outward movement of a production possibility surface. Similarly the relative importance of the components of national income can be interpreted in terms of their relative satisfaction or cost to the economy. Thus the indicator of economic welfare must be some national accounts measure.

But the quality of the statistics in developing countries is poor, and the conversion into a common currency at actual exchange rates produces some ridiculous results. Bacon and Beckerman therefore re-estimate the national accounts measure of per capita consumption, using non-monetary indicators. The procedure was to start with 'corrected' measures of consumption per head as estimated by Gilbert and associates for nine developed countries, and by other authors for the USSR, China, India and Japan. These 'corrected' measures of per capita consumption were then correlated with a large number of non-monetary indicators such as cement produced, stock of radios and telephones, and so on, for the relevant countries. By a process of trial and error a particular form of equation was found which combined a group of these indicators in such a way that they were closely correlated with the 'corrected' values of per capita consumption. The final stage was to use the coefficients of these indicators to re-estimate the real level of per capita consumption of as many countries as have data on these non-monetary indicators.

The crucial assumption of this method is that for these five or six indicators the Engel curves relating expenditure on major items of consumption to income are virtually identical in every country and are very insensitive to inter-country differences in relative prices. This was certainly the case for the author's 13 countries, with values estimated for 1950 and 1955, but only eight of the 26 observations (two for each country) were for underdeveloped countries, and four of these observations were for the USSR and Japan. While it continues to be necessary to re-estimate national accounts the question will remain, whether the assumption regarding the position of the Engel curves is universally valid for the rest of the world. Meanwhile the approach put forward by Bacon and Beckerman must rank as a valuable advance in the study of the process of developments.

1.5 The accuracy of statistics in developing countries

This brief survey of international comparisons reflects a basic problem in studying developing countries, the paucity and inaccuracy of statistics. The most accurate statistics are probably those for foreign trade because there are only a few outlets capable of handling these goods and the flows can therefore be easily recorded. In addition a fair proportion of government revenues come from taxes on foreign trade and thus detailed records are kept. A large and increasing proportion of government revenues in LDCs are derived from taxes on internal transactions (see chapter 3) but evasion of these taxes is much easier. Statistics of the value of output which are based on the expenditure side of the national accounts will therefore seriously underestimate the true total. Possibly the most inaccurate statistics are those of population, particularly on vital issues such as birth rates, age of mother at birth of the child, age of marriage, age at death, and so on. For example when the UN was recently compiling statistics on infant mortality rates for the period 1947-55 they found only six countries in the whole of Asia and Africa with relatively good figures of this important indicator. Since these six included Israel, Japan, Singapore, and South Africa the sample could hardly be said to be representative of underdeveloped countries as a whole (see McGranahan). There is a short discussion on the use and interpretation of population statistics in chapter two, and for the moment we will concentrate on the conceptual and practical problems of drawing up a system of national accounts in a developing country.

1.6 Measuring the national income of a developing country

What is the purpose of drawing up a set of national accounts and how much scarce resources of skilled manpower should be devoted to this task? Much will be known about the structure of the economy from other sources such as the census of population, trade statistics and so on. However when for example there is rapid structural change from primary industry towards manufacturing industry, results in a growing demand for social overhead capital, additional information is required, not only on the structure of the economy but also on the economic costs and benefits of this change. The government needs this information to frame its economic policy. It is sometimes stated that developing countries should produce simple, not detailed, accounts because of the paucity of records and shortage of skilled manpower. However the counter argument is that this would only produce 'large shapes in a thick fog' and that by giving precise detail on particular points the overall accuracy of the picture will be improved.

The national accounts are of course drawn up from the three points of income (remuneration of factors of production), output (value added), and expenditure (consumption and investment). Provided all three are consistently defined it should be possible to calculate each independently and arrive at the same answer. In practice the nature of the data will dictate that the accounts will be derived primarily from one method of computation, the other two methods acting as a cross check on this one. In a developed country income tax returns and social security records usually provide the main basis for the accounts. In a developing country income levels are too low for a widespread income tax to be an economic proposition. Similarly on the expenditure side there are usually inadequate statistics on family budgets to assess private consumption. The national accounts therefore rely heavily on the output side. In all three methods the underdeveloped state of the economy creates fundamental practical and conceptual problems.

Practical problems refer to the difficulty of obtaining information. People do not keep records of transactions because they have no need to or because they are unable to do so through lack of education. Sample surveys may help but these are very costly in their use of skilled manpower and there are technical difficulties derived from ignorance of the size and character of the 'population' to be sampled.[1] In addition there are difficulties in obtaining accurate replies even when skilled interviewers are used. People may not understand the questions or may deliberately give wrong answers. Thus if they suspect that questions on the value of output are being asked for the purpose of levying a tax they will tend to understate their true production. On the other hand if they think the information will be used to evaluate compensation under a land reform and consolidation programme they may considerably overstate the value of output produced. Sample surveys are often the only

1 For a discussion of this, see C W Howse.

means of obtaining vitally important information for development planning but the results must be treated with great caution.

The most intractable problems are those concerned with conceptual issues. In all national accounts there is the fundamental difficulty of measuring all production in terms of money. In developed countries the question of whether to give an imputed value to wives' housework is peripheral; in an underdeveloped country it becomes central. The 'family' is an important source of labour and some value must be placed on this, but should the prevailing wage rate for unskilled labour be used?

Another source of difficulty is that the process of development can give a value to goods which at an earlier stage of development had no scarcity value. An example of this is housing, which costs virtually nothing in the subsistence economy because materials and labour are mostly given free. However in an urban setting housing has an important economic value. By including the value of urban housing in the accounts but excluding rural housing the rate of development of the economy will be exaggerated. But how is it possible to impute a value to housing in the subsistence sector? Phyllis Deane has also pointed out that traditional societies often have complicated gift patterns which cannot be identified as payments for particular goods and services.

The really major conceptual difficulty concerns the imputed value of the subsistence sector. To omit the value of output produced and consumed by the traditional farmer would be grossly to underestimate the value of economic activity in the country. But even if reasonably reliable estimates of physical output can be produced using sample surveys there remains the problem of placing a value on this output. What meaning can be placed on the ruling market price of a commodity when it is known that most of the output of this commodity does not appear on the market? Clearly this is not an equilibrium price. Even if it is felt that market prices are a reasonable approximation to the value of the output, which market price should be used, producers' price, wholesale price or retail price? Retail prices include a service element for marketing and distribution; producers' prices may underestimate the true scarcity value because of local monopsony powers. As Barber points out the prices used are certainly not the neutral ones of revealed preference and tell us rather about the value judgements of the person drawing up the accounts!

A similar criticism can be levelled at the attempt to force the economic activity of a developing country into a Keynesian framework. Decisions on what to include or exclude, such as the services of witch doctors or chieftains, are often viewed in terms of how they fit into a 'western' concept of economic activity. The use of Keynesian concepts of consumption, investment and saving have also been criticised. For instance in traditional agriculture decisions to invest or consume are taken by one and the same person not by separate groups of people. Even increased consumption of food cannot be interpreted in Keynesian terms. At low levels of food intake additional consumption of food will appreciably increase the productive power of the individual and in this sense can be viewed as investment. Similarly the classification of expenditure on health and education as 'consumption' is highly misleading. In the context of a developing country it is much more useful to regard such expenditure as investment which contributes to development by improving the quality of labour.

The purpose of this discussion has not been to turn the reader entirely away from the use of statistics, for unless theories about the nature of the development process and the causes of success and failure in the past are quantified there will be little progress. What must be emphasised is a proper scepticism in the use and interpretation of the statistics. It is in the nature of economics that a proposition can never be proved beyond all question and this is particularly true when dealing with unreliable data.

1.7 Dualism in developing countries
The absence of information on the distribution of the aggregates has been mentioned as one of the problems in trying to draw a statistical picture of a developing country. One important example of this is the common characteristic of *dualism* in developing countries.

The term dualism has come to have a number of meanings but basically it refers to a persistent and increasing gap, on an international level between developed and less developed countries, and within developing countries between the advanced, modern exchange sector emphasising relatively large-scale units and the rest of the economy. Recent analysis has particularly focused on the latter phenomenon because this increasing divergence between the two sectors within a single country is both striking and puzzling to the observer, and dangerous to future development.

This sharp contrast between the modern and traditional sectors of a developing country has been explained in terms of a contrast in social values, between capitalism imported from the west and traditional 'eastern' values. The most famous exposition of this thesis is by Boeke who sees a clash between capitalist ideas of unlimited needs and 'eastern' concepts of limited needs. Thus the traditional sector is characterised by backward-sloping supply curves of effort and risk taking. These ideas have been sharply criticised by many economists with wide experience in developing countries, and are probably best summarised by Higgins. Complex institutional factors appear to retard development but these barriers are not immutable. Indeed developing countries may abandon traditional values all too readily and accept some of the less desirable aspects of 'western' life. Orthodox economic theory therefore seems to be still a useful tool of analysis in developing countries, provided it is modified by making assumptions appropriate to the institutions of the area.

Modern theories of dualism therefore concentrate on an economic interpretation of the problem. Dualism is puzzling not because a contrast exists between the modern and traditional, for this is only to be expected, but because the gap is widening. As the modern sector expands, one would expect the techniques and principles of the market economy to spread throughout the whole economy. As the modern sector draws in more labour from agriculture so traditional farmers should be induced to produce cash crops for sale. In addition to drawing an increasing part of the economy into the exchange sector this shift towards cash crops, added to the migration of labour from agriculture, should induce changes in techniques of production and encourage specialisation and hence further exchange. In this way the gap between the modern and traditional sectors should narrow over time. In fact the modern sector has enormously expanded while the traditional sector has progressed only slowly. Why has this occurred?

One explanation centres on the nature of the modern sector which was typically established during the colonial era to meet the needs of the 'western' country. The modern sector consisted of mines, plantations and later oil fields, all using highly capital intensive techniques of production. It followed that this sector was in essence a foreign enclave with practically no links with the traditional sector. The capital goods were imported and what little labour was required was mostly highly skilled and therefore brought over from the investing country. On the other hand, one of the benefits of colonialism was gradually to introduce western knowledge of medicine and public health and this, combined with the effect of colonial rule in reducing internal wars, caused an increase in the rate of growth of population. Virtually the whole of this faster increase in the labour force had to find employment in the agricultural sector. Land became scarcer and labour increasingly abundant. Since techniques of production were very flexible in agriculture, unlike the rigid coefficients of industry, production processes became more labour intensive and output per man fell. Broadly speaking this is the explanation of *technological dualism* proposed by Eckaus.

The mere existence of two contrasting sectors is not significant. Clearly this contrast will exist so long as the economy is underdeveloped. But an increase of 'dualism' means that the resources available to the economy have been wrongly allocated. In the past this may have been caused by colonialism, whose objective was to develop the colonising country not the underdeveloped country. Today, as Myint and Singer argue, dualism has mostly been the result of misguided government policies and the 'backwash' effects of the rapid growth of the developed countries.

Government policies in developing countries aimed at accelerating growth through industrialisation have aggravated already unequal access to economic resources. For example, to encourage industrialisation, governments have provided firms with capital at unrealistically low rates of interest. The corollary is that capital is made even scarcer in the agricultural sector and consequently rates of interest here are far higher than should be the case. Other forms of encouragement of industry are high protective tariffs, preferential access to social overhead capital and overvalued exchange rates. The latter enable firms to import capital goods at unrealistically low prices. As is emphasised in chapter 3 the result of over-expansion of industry and under-expansion of agriculture is inflation. The combination of inflation, overvalued exchange rates and low interest rates results in capital flight and if this is blocked then the capital goes into unproductive forms.

An additional feature of the dual economy is the relatively high level of wages in the industrial sector which cannot be wholly explained by genuine differences in skills or by the higher cost of living in urban areas. The cause is partly minimum wage regulations but also the activities of strong unions who tend to use wage awards in foreign-owned export industries as a lever to force up wages in the whole industrial sector. The effect of this is to encourage industries to select more capital intensive techniques of production and to discourage the growth of more labour intensive industries.

It is this last effect that Singer describes as the 'backwash' effect of the rapid expansion of the developed countries. In particular he emphasises that the vast bulk of research in science and technology is concentrated in the developed countries and reflects the factor proportions existing in these countries. Skilled people 'brain drain' away from the developing to the developed countries, and the developed countries are mostly concerned to advance technologies quite inappropriate to the needs of the developing countries.

Little research has been conducted in developing countries to determine the extent to which small scale industries can be established and encouraged to provide a rapid growth of employment and still use capital efficiently. What little research has been carried out however is not encouraging, for labour intensive techniques often have high capital-output ratios. Since capital is usually the limiting factor of production there may well appear to be a dilemma between promoting the growth of output and the growth of employment. There are in fact many possibilities in the agricultural sector of raising the growth of both output and employment as described in chapter 3. However to the extent that the dilemma exists there is a strong case for innovations which will absorb labour and also use capital efficiently. One of the most pressing social needs of developing countries is to reduce the open unemployment in urban areas, frequently as high as 15 to 20 per cent, and at the same time reduce the flow of labour attracted by high wages from agriculture to the urban areas by raising the productivity, and therefore the earnings, of labour in agriculture. At the same time strategies for accelerating growth through import substitution need to be re-examined.

references and further reading

R Bacon and W Beckerman   'The international comparisons of income levels: a suggested new measurement.' *Economic Journal* 1966

W J Barber   'A critique of aggregate accounts concepts in under-developed areas', *Bulletin of the Oxford Institute of Economics and Statistics* 1963

J H Boeke   Economics and economic policy of dual societies, New York 1953

H B Chenery   'Patterns of industrial growth' *American Economic Review* September 1960

C Clark   *The conditions of economic progress*, London: Macmillan 1940

C Clark   *The economics of subsistence agriculture*, London: Macmillan 1964

P Deane   *The measurement of colonial national accounts*, Cambridge UP 1948

R S Eckaus   'The factor proportions problem in underdeveloped areas', *American Economic Review*, 1955

M Gilbert and associates   *Comparative national products and price levels*, Paris, OEEC, 1958

M Gilbert and I B Kravis   *An international comparison of national products and the purchasing power of currencies*, OEEC, 1954

B Higgins   'The dualistic theory of underdeveloped areas', *Economic Development and Cultural Change* 1956

C W Howse   'Use of sample household expenditure surveys in economic planning in East Africa', *Bulletin of the Oxford Institute of Economics and Statistics*, 1966

S Kuznets   'Quantitative aspects of the economic growth of nations, *Economic Development and Cultural Change* July 1957

D V McGranahan   'Comparative social research in the United Nations', in R L Merritt and S Rokkan (ed) *Comparing Nations* New Haven and London: Yale UP 1966

H Myint   'Dualism and the internal integration of the under-developed countries', *Banco Nazionale del Lavaro Quarterly Review* June 1970 No.93

L Pearson   *Partners in development*, London: Pall Mall 1969

H Singer   'Dualism revisited : a new approach to the problems of the
                            dual society in developing countries', *Journal of
                            Development Studies* 1970
UNESCO   *Social aspects of economic development in Latin
                            America* Vol 1 Paris 1963 reproduced in Higgins *Economic
                            Development* (2nd Ed.) London : Constable 1968

For a full exposition of national income accounting see the first volume in the series:

D Croome and J N Robinson *Understanding the economy : an introduction to
                            macroeconomic theory* London: Weidenfeld and
                            Nicolson 1972 Ch 2.

chapter 2

the population explosion and economic development

'No other phenomenon casts a darker shadow over the prospects for international development than the staggering growth of population'.

2.1 Introduction

Perhaps this view, taken from the Pearson Report, is an over dramatic one of the situation, but it is generally agreed that the only hope of reducing the relative gap between rich and poor countries is for the latter to reduce their growth of population. For instance during the last decade the average growth of output has been roughly the same for both groups of countries, 4·8 to 5·0 per cent per annum, but output per head increased by an average of 3·6 per cent per annum for developed countries but only 2·5 per cent per annum for the less developed countries. It is therefore tempting to draw the conclusion that if only the rate of growth of population had been lower then, given the same output, the per capita incomes of the developing countries would have been appreciably improved. However such a view is not only a considerable oversimplification of the problem but is also misleading in that it poses the issue as either increasing the rate of growth of domestic output or decreasing the rate of growth of population. In fact the growth of output and population are not independently determined and it is essential to examine their interrelationship in a dynamic context.

Before examining the economic case for population limitation it is necessary to obtain some perspective on the problem and briefly consider some of the factors underlying the increasing rates of growth of population and the prospects of these rates being maintained in the future.

2.2 The growth in population since 1950

The rate of growth of population in LDCs has tended to increase from about 2·2 per cent per annum in the period 1950-60 to 2·5 per cent per annum in 1960-9. This acceleration was a result of the maintenance of high rates of increase, 3 per cent per annum, in Latin America and the Middle East, and an increase in rates in South Asia from 2 per cent to over 2·5 per cent per annum as shown in table 3.

Table 3
The growth of the world population 1950-69

	1950	1960	1969	% Increase 1950-60	% Increase 1960-69
World	2,517	3,005	3,552	2·0%	1·9%
Africa	222	278	345	2·3	2·4
Latin America	163	213	276	2·8	2·9
South Asia	697	866	1,087	1·9	2·6
Europe	392	425	460	0·8	0·9

Source UN Demographic Yearbook 1969

This acceleration in population growth rates has been the net result of rates of mortality falling faster than those for births, as shown in table 4.

Table 4
Mortality and fertility rates in selected countries

	growth of population 1963-9 per cent per annum	infant mortality rate per 1000 live births 1945-9	1969	expectation of life at birth 1960-5 males	females	fertility rate births per 1000 females aged 10 – 49 (1965)
Mauritius	2·2	143	64	59	62	134·6
UAR	2·5	139	118·5	52	54	150
Jamaica	2·4	90	35·2	63	67	144·3
Argentina	1·5	74	60	63	69	75·7
Chile	2·4	150	91	54	60	104·4
Ceylon	2·4	110·5	47·7	62	61	122
Japan	1·1	67	14	69	74	56·4
W. Malaysia	2·8	91	45	63	66	122·3
Pakistan	2·1	138	142	54	49	247
Phillipines	3·5	101·5	72	na	na	89·6
UK	0·6		18·8	69	75	65·4
USA	1·2		21	67	74	61·6

Source UN Demographic Yearbooks

For instance in many developing countries the expectation of life at birth in the period 1942-6 was only about 30 to 35 years. Today outside tropical Africa it would be exceptional to find a country with a life expectancy of less than 45 years for males and 48 years for females, while a number of countries record figures of 60 years and over. Infant mortality rates have varied very considerably since 1950 since they are highly sensitive to certain public health measures, but in many cases have fallen dramatically from rates of 100 − 150 down to 35 − 65 per thousand live births. This dramatic fall in mortality rates has been the result above all of public health measures imported from the developed countries.

Trends in fertility rates are more difficult to determine because of the paucity of information but it is certain that there has been nothing like the decline that has occurred in mortality rates. In almost every developing country rates still exceed 100 and in some cases reach levels of 200 or more, compared to rates of 56 for Japan and 60 to 65 for the United States and Britain. As would be expected, countries with the highest increase in population show the greatest difference between fertility rates and life expectancy at birth.

It is worth noting that when illustrating the large differential movements which have occurred in natality and mortality in the post-war period it is not correct to use the crude birth and death rates − the number of births and deaths each year per thousand of the total population. Both these and particularly the birth rate are highly sensitive to the age and sex structure of the population. For example if more women are entering the reproductive age groups the crude birth rate will increase even though fertility rates have remained constant. Similarly if there is an ageing structure of population the crude death rates will rise over time even though people may be living longer. Thus the crude death rate for the UK is 11·9, almost as high as that for many LDCs.

Of course actual methods of analysis will depend on the quality and availability of demographic statistics. There is for instance considerable doubt about the size of the total population of many countries particularly those of Africa, and vital statistics of age, number of births etc must be treated with a great deal of caution. This is not surprising considéring the elaborate administrative structure and scarce skills required to carry out a census, particularly if the population is mostly illiterate and scattered over a wide area often linked by only rudimentary transport and communications. The UN have assisted evaluation by classifying information according to a *quality code* (see the *Demographic Yearbook* 1969 pp 7-12) based on an annual questionnaire on methods of collection and coverage of data. The data can also be compared to 'model' statistics[1] but the usefulness of this method is limited by ignorance of what is credible. These factors, among numerous others, must be borne in mind when considering the factors determining the future growth of the populations of developing countries.

1 Values which could reasonably be expected based on past experience.

2.3 The theory of demographic transition

In order to make projections of the rate of growth of population, its age composition, etc there must be a theory to isolate and determine the relationships between key variables. Fundamentally this theory assumes that parents have a desired family size, the size being determined not only by the happiness derived from children but also by the economic needs of the parents. For instance the need for a supply of labour on the family plot of land and to provide for the parents in their old age. It is assumed that parents weigh the costs of an additional child against these benefits. The total cost includes both the obvious costs of maintaining the children, especially in the early years when they will consume more than they produce, and the hidden costs arising from such factors as the decreased ability of the mother to work through childbearing and caring for the children and the decreased mobility of the parents.

In the initial stages of development when techniques of agricultural production are primitive and most if not all the labour comes from the family, the economic benefits from children will be high and they will only slowly diminish as the family increases in size. Similarly children will be an important source of security for the parents in their old age. Direct costs of maintaining the children in this primitive state will be low, and indirect costs probably negligible. Under these conditions the desired family size will be high and given the probably high mortality rate of children it follows that fertility rates will also be high.

As economic development proceeds and the productivity of labour rises with changes in techniques of production and the application of more capital, the desired size of family falls. Children become less important as a source of labour, and as incomes rise so parents are increasingly able to save and provide for their old age. At the same time, as the benefits from children diminish, so probably will their costs rise since not only do they share in the general increase in consumption standards but they are also unproductive for a greater number of years following the introduction of elementary education.

The process of development also involves increased migration from rural to urban locations and urbanization plays an important part in the theory. Large families are seen as a disadvantage because they limit the mobility of the parents, restrict the gainful employment of the mother as well as directly increasing costs by necessitating larger accommodation and hence higher rents where previously housing was probably a free good. Urbanization will also directly reduce fertility rates by assisting the disintegration of social customs such as early marriages, which are conducive to large families. Thus with a reduced desired size of family and lower mortality rates resulting from higher standards of living, rapid declines in fertility rates may be expected.

It is however not expected that the fall in fertility rates will take place simultaneously with the decline in mortality rates, for realisation of a permanent decline in mortality and a continuing increase in incomes will not be immediate. So the initial impact of rising standards of living will probably be an acceleration in the rate of growth of population as fertility remains constant, or even rises, while mortality particularly of infants rapidly declines. Fertility rates decline only slowly because social customs change slowly in response to economic development. Meanwhile the abandonment of these customs imposes considerable social cost on the individual.

The theory does not postulate any rigid relationship between per capita incomes and rates of growth of population. To postulate such a rigid relationship would be an analysis of despair since it would imply that high rates of growth of population would continue indefinitely and condemn such countries for ever to low levels and rates of growth of income. Leibenstein and Nelson have produced models along these lines, and inevitably arrive at the conclusion that the only successful development policy is one of sudden and massive expansion of the economy to raise the income growth curve suddenly above that of population and thus place the economy on a self-sustaining growth path. Myint has severely criticised these models, arguing that the necessity for a 'critical minimum effort' arises only from the unrealistic assumption of the model. Such may well be the case but it seems reasonable to assume that some relationship does exist between fertility rates and both the level and the rate of growth of per capita incomes, as well as between fertility and mortality rates.

Evidence on these relationships is scarce and often conflicting but an interesting study has been carried out by Caldwell on fertility attitudes in three economically contrasting rural regions of Ghana. This study demonstrated that as economic development proceeded, and with it the introduction of a cash economy and elementary education, so the desire for smaller families was strengthened even among people with such deeply entrenched high fertility traditions as the Ashanti. However other cross-section studies of a number of countries, notably by Adelman and Weintraub, do not support the theory and instead find a positive relationship between fertility trends and per capita real income, though most of their results were not statistically significant. Perhaps the evidence by Krishnamurty for India in the period 1922-60 presents the correct perspective. In this study the birth rate was related to per capita real income and a time trend, this being a catch-all variable summarising all trends that would reduce the birth rate, such as urbanisation, increased education, etc. These variables explained *50 per cent* of the variations in the birth rate, and the income coefficient implied that a one per cent increase in per capita real income would induce a slightly less than proportional fall in the birth rate. Also of interest was the finding that a one per cent increase in per capita real incomes would induce a 1·8 per cent fall in the death rate, thus illustrating the predicted lag between these two vital rates.

2.4 The basis for population projections

There are many unknown variables influencing desired family size and the rate of fertility decline, and little knowledge about factors affecting the size of the time lag between falling death and birth rates, and the critical rate of growth, as well as the level of per capita income at which induced fertility decline will begin. But despite these uncertainties some intelligent guesses can be made about the future composition and growth of population, if only because a growing population has its own momentum. For example it is inevitable that the majority of today's daughters will become tomorrow's mothers, and, depending on future fertility and mortality rates, they will in turn provide the basis for future generations. The basis for such projections is the *gross reproduction rate:* the number of live daughters that a woman would give birth to during her reproductive life span at current age specific fertility rates. This figure is 'gross' because it does not allow for mortality of females below the age of 50, that is, the gross reproduction rate effectively indicate the upper limit to the future rate of growth of population provided there is no substantial increase in fertility rates.

If this gross rate is corrected for female mortality, the *net reproduction rate* is calculated. If the net rate is unity the population is simply replacing itself at current rates of fertility and mortality, and growth is zero.

Information is naturally more plentiful on gross than net rates (in the 1969 *Demographic Yearbook,* 97 countries reported gross rates and only 57 net rates), but even allowing for the fact that gross rates represent the upper limit for future growth, they are still alarmingly high in many countries; somewhere in the region of 2·3 to 3·7. Given the rapid increase in life expectancy, it could be argued that this potential rate of growth could well be close to the actual one, if one assumed unchanged fertility rates. Such an assumption would be invalid, because fertility rates will be directly affected by changes in the age of marriage, the desired family size, effectiveness in controlling births, and so on.

These factors can be predicted by examining changes in *age specific fertility rates* over time, that is, the number of live births to women in particular age groups. Additional information on future trends may be provided by considering the rate of urbanisation, for in many countries, though by no means all, the child-women ratio is appreciably lower in urban than in rural areas. This could of course be due to the younger age structure of the female population of these areas and simply mean that they have not completed their families, but it may also be brought about by lower fertility rates. The UN in 1969 estimated that in the less developed regions the agglomerated population, defined as those living in towns greater than 20,000 people, had increased fourfold in the previous 40 years, and they expected this rate to continue for the next 40 years. This projection has some sobering implications, but it might well contribute to lower fertility rates and hence to a lower overall population growth.

Another related factor which must be taken into account when making projections of fertility rates is the possibility of an increase in the age of brides. For instance, in Jordan, Tunisia, and the UAR more than 50 per cent of brides are aged under 19, as against 25 per cent for the UK, which is itself high by European standards; while the UN mission to India in 1965 estimated that by 1975, of 9 million prevented births, 1·9 million could result from a rise in the age of marriage. As Taeuber (1958) has shown, part of the decline in the growth of the Japanese population was due to the postponement and a reduced overall rate of marriage. For example, in 1920, 85 per cent of women aged 24 and under were married; by 1955 this figure had fallen to 36 per cent. Similarly the history of population growth in western Europe in the nineteenth century and early twentieth century, particularly in countries such as France and Ireland, seems to indicate that where a larger family is seen as undesirable the means to limit the size of family will generally be found.

The present increase in population of developing countries is, of course, greater and has occurred in markedly different circumstances than prevailed in western Europe in the nineteenth century. Also as Taeuber (1969) points out Japan is certainly a special case, and even here the determination of most families to have only two children came after a century of rapid industrialisation and urbanisation. Nevertheless, to look at the historical experience of countries with markedly different cultures does act as a corrective to the point of view which regards population control solely in terms of providing the methods of and 'education' on how to limit families. Fundamentally, it appears that parents will only regard a larger family as undesirable when it conflicts with clearly perceived opportunities for socio-economic advancement. Only when this prior condition is fulfilled will family planning programmes play a part in the general move towards smaller families.

2.5 The population of developing countries to the year 2,000
In considering projections for the world's population for the next 30 years it is worth noting that demographers are always careful to draw a distinction between prediction, which they never make, and projections, which are simply the mathematical result of making certain assumptions about movements in key variables over a period of time.

A projection most widely referred to is that by the UN, *World population prospects as assessed in 1963.* In this study the general assumption was made that the decline in mortality experienced during the 1950s would continue with life expectancy increasing by two and a half years in each quinquennium until the age of 55, then rising at a slightly faster rate to the age of 65 and then slowing down to reach a limit of 74. Similarly a general assumption was made that fertility would decline by 50 per cent over a 30 year period; but, in the case of developing countries a number of different assumptions were made with regard to the initial year in which this fertility decline would begin. Thus by varying the onset of the decline in fertility *high, medium* and *low* projections of population were produced to the year 2000. Considerable effort was put into determining plausible boundaries for these initial years, each region and sometimes individual countries being studied separately in the light of the best available knowledge. For example in the case of tropical Africa no major decline in fertility was expected, indeed in the *high* projection an increase in fertility was assumed, while in the *low* case, mortality was assumed to fall by only half the rate assumed elsewhere.

Table 5
Estimated world population, 1960 – 2000 (millions)

5(a) as assessed in 1963

		High		Medium		Low	
	1960	1980	2000	1980	2000	1980	2000
World	2,998	4,551	6,994	4,330	6,130	4,147	5,449
More developed areas	854	1,086	1,317	1,043	1,266	1,006	1,129
Less developed areas	2,144	3,465	5,677	3,287	4,864	3,141	4,320
Mainland China	654	971	1,345	850	1,045	782	893
Japan	93	117	139	111	122	108	115
Other East Asia	47	83	139	80	120	76	110
South Asia	865	1,448	2,444	1,420	2,270	1,378	1,984
Africa	273	463	864	449	768	434	684
Latin America	212	383	686	378	638	362	532

Source UN World population prospects as assessed in 1963 New York 1966

5(b) revised estimates 1971 medium variant

			Annual growth of population		
	1980	2000	1963-70	1970-85	1970-2000
World	4,457	6,494	2·0	2·0	2·0
More developed areas	1,210	1,453	1·0	1·0	–
Less developed areas	3,247	5,040	2·4	2·4	–
Mainland China	894	1,165	1·8	1·6	1·4
Japan	116	133	1·1	1·0	0·9
Other East Asia	77	115	2·6	2·4	2·2
South Asia	1,486	2,354	2·7	2·7	2·5
Africa	457	818	2·5	2·9	2·9
Latin America	377	652	2·9	2·9	2·8

Source UN Monthly Bulletin of Statistics April 1971

The results are summarised in table 5(a). Even in the case of rapid fertility decline there is not an appreciably lower size of population by 1980 compared to the variant of *high* fertility. This illustrates what Ohlin refers to as the *braking distance* of a population: the increase in numbers resulting from the inability to switch immediately to the lower growth rate. Thus in the *high* projection the rate of growth of population only begins to fall in 1990. However by the year 2000 the *high* projection for the developing countries produces a size of population which is more than 50 per cent larger than the *low* projection.

Table 5(b) gives revised (1971) estimates of this projection in the light of improved information on key variables and shows significant increases in the medium variant, particularly for mainland China but also for Africa and to a lesser extent South Asia in the year 2000.

2.6 The economists' case for population control
The economic case for limiting the growth of population in developing countries is by no means obvious. Arguments that the problem is one of feeding or of providing employment for underemployed agricultural labour or the large and rapidly increasing army of urban unemployed, are forms of special pleading and as such do not form a useful basis for analysis. Economists ·are not unanimous in regarding the growth of population as an unmitigated curse. Colin Clark suggests that the pressure of population can often act as a forcing house for social and economic change; techniques of agricultural production are improved, swamps are drained and uncultivated land cleared. Hirschman similarly sees the pressure of population as a useful stimulant providing profitable investment opportunities and fostering entrepreneurial skill and risk taking, since the risk of failure is reduced by the expanding market. The advantages of a larger market are also well documented referring particularly to the creation of economies of scale both internal and external through the growth of a skilled labour force, the provision of specialised services and generally through complementarities on both the supply and demand[1] sides. Economies of scale are particularly obvious in the provision of social overhead capital, communications, public health, education and so on.

Why has India such a low level of per capita income if the pressure of population is so beneficial? Colin Clark forestalls such a question by claiming that India has prevented this process from taking place in agriculture by land reform policies and by keeping food prices artificially low through a policy of rationing and cheap imports. Presumably he would also regard the technological advances of the *green revolution* as

1 In the sense that goods entering into mass consumption provide a market for each other through the growth of incomes.

another result of population pressure. Finally he quotes Suavy 'if population limitation were the key to economic progress then France would be the richest country in the world'. This is a good debating point but it is not claimed that population limitation is the key to economic development, only that the rapid *growth* of population makes the acceleration of growth of output per head more difficult. The present experience of developing countries has no historical precedent and a rapid growth of their populations could well have a detrimental effect on their rate of capital accumulation.

This dynamic relationship is also ignored by those who regard tropical Africa and most of Latin America as 'obviously' underpopulated and Asia as 'obviously' overpopulated. Implicit in this approach is the concept of some optimum size of population in relation to resources of land, with density used as an indicator for this relationship. Apart from the fact that there is no systematic relationship between density and income per head the concept of such an optimum is meaningless. If it is assumed that in LDCs the rate of capital accumulation is inversely related to the rate of growth of population, it follows that the static optimum size of population will change as the population grows. In other words the concept of some optimum size of population has no meaning since the necessary *ceteris paribus* assumption can never be made.

In stressing the relationship between population growth, capital accumulation and economic development it is not suggested that capital accumulation on its own is a sufficient condition for economic development, merely that it is a necessary condition without which even the most potentially productive areas of the world cannot be developed.

Why should the rate of capital accumulation be inversely related to the rate of growth of population? Under present conditions the rate of growth of population in developing countries is directly determined by the gap between fertility and mortality rates. An increase in life expectancy, although initially having the greater impact on children, eventually affects all age groups. High fertility rates on the other hand have the sole effect of increasing the number of children in the population. It follows that those developing countries which have high rates of growth of population also have a large proportion of children in the population, and the higher the absolute value of fertility rates the greater this proportion. Bourgeois-Pichat has calculated that in the less developed countries as a whole, for every 100 productive adults there are 85 non-productive people comprising 79 children and 6 adults. Conversely for the developed countries the proportion is 57, 36 children and 21 adults.

It must be emphasised however that this *burden of dependency* in LDCs critically depends on which age groups are included as part of the labour force and in particular on the treatment of the age group 10 to 14 years. Some illustrations are given in table 6.

Table 6
Two measures of the burden of dependency in LDCs

	Census Year	Dependency Burden 'A'	Dependency Burden 'A'
Mauritius	1968	0·94	0·50
UAR	1960	0·95	0·53
Ghana	1960	0·98	0·60
Kenya	1962	1·05	0·81
Jamaica	1960	0·92	0·51
Argentina	1960	0·66	0·37
Brazil	1960	0·90	0·50
Chile	1968	0·87	0·51
Ceylon	1963	0·91	0·50
India	1961	0·88	0·49
Pakistan	1961	1·02	0·62
UK	1969	0·54	
USA	1969	0·63	

Source UN Demographic Yearbook 1969,

Notes   Dependency burden 'A' $=$ $\dfrac{(0\text{-}14) + (60+)}{(15\text{-}59)}$

Dependency burden 'B' $=$ $\dfrac{(0\text{-}9) + (65+)}{(10\text{-}64)}$

Dependency burden for
UK and US $\dfrac{(0\text{-}14) + (65+)}{(15\text{-}64)}$

Despite this qualification it is clear that developing countries experiencing a rapid growth of population will have an unfavourable age structure of population. In addition population dynamics carry considerable momentum and the age structure of a population will respond very slowly to a change in fertility. Fertility rates in any case are falling very slowly if at all, so the unfavourable age composition will inevitably continue for at least the next few generations.

Coale constructs an illustrative projection of a population with an initial growth rate of three per cent per annum, an expectation of life of 53 years which will rise to 70 over the next 30 years, and an average initial family size of six children. Two assumptions are then made about fertility. In projection A current fertility rates continue unchanged, while in projection B they fall by two per cent per annum over the next 25 years. Clearly for the first 15 years there will be no difference in the numbers of working age in the two projections. The whole impact of decreased fertility in B will result in a decreased proportion of children in the population. It follows that during this first 15 years output per head in B will certainly be higher not only because of a lower denominator but probably because total output will itself be higher. The labour force may well be larger due to the increased participation of women, a factor which will be particularly important where agricultural output critically depends on seasonal inputs of labour. Also as consumption standards rise with increased per capita output, the productivity of labour may increase as well. Furthermore an increased proportion of national output may be channelled into directly productive investment instead of into the replication of social capital to meet the needs of the increased population of A.

After 15 years the comparison of the economic effects of the two projections becomes more complex. Starting in about 20 years there develops at first a slight and then a widening difference in the population of working age so that after 60 years the working population of A is double that of B. Thereafter A's population of working age increases at about 3·5 per cent per annum and B's at just over one per cent per annum. Against this it must be remembered that the burden of dependency will continue to rise in A despite the increase in those of working age and fall in B, as the cumulative effects of high and low fertility rates work their way through to subsequent generations of parents. Thus from an initial level of 190, A's dependency burden will rise to 200 in a period of 60 years, while in B it will fall to 160 in the same period. Thereafter the proportions will remain constant though this still implies a widening absolute gap in the number of children in the two projections.

To summarise this illustrative projection:

Model:
Initial size of population 1 million.
Initial growth of population 3 per cent.
Initial expectation of life 53 years.
Initial desired family size 6 children.

Expectation of life increases to 70 years over the next thirty years.
Two projections of fertility A — fertility unchanged.
B — falls by 50 per cent over 25 years.

Results:

After 20 years:

		Projection A	Projection B
1	0 – 14	870,000	637,000
2	15 – 64	996,000	985,000
3	Total population	1·9 million	1·7 million
4	Investment in social capital	Increase	Constant
5	Investment in productive capital	Fall	Increase
6	Per capita consumption	Constant/Fall	Increase

After 60 years:

1	0 – 14	3·8 million	1·0 million
2	15 – 64	4·2 million	2·2 million
3	Total population	8·3 million	3·4 million

2.7 Conclusions
A complex model such as that used for India and Mexico by Coale and Hoover is illustrated in Figure 1 showing the relationships between the growth of population and social and economic variables. Central place is given to fertility rates since under present conditions in most developing countries the crucial elements of the growth of population and the *dependency burden* are principally determined by the age specific fertility rates. It must be emphasised that knowledge of the nature and magnitude of the determinants of fertility rates is very imperfect. However it seems possible that fertility rates are primarily determined by mortality rates, particularly infant mortality rates, and by the level and distribution of per capita income. There is however a lag between an increase in per capita incomes and a fall in mortality rates and a consequent fall in fertility. This lag is partly determined by the time required to break down institutional forces such as early marriage conducive to high fertility and appropriate to an era of high mortality. The lag is also determined by the time required for the realisation that circumstances have changed and that the additional child now imposes a substantial economic cost on the parents. In this respect a rapid growth of incomes may serve to jolt people into the realisation that conditions have improved. In addition the lag may be shortened by education and urbanisation causing an acceleration in the abandonment of inappropriate customs. In the past public health programmes have had the exclusive effect of reducing mortality, but it is hoped that they can also operate directly on fertility rates by means of birth control programmes. It is however an open question whether any appreciable and lasting results will be achieved by such measured in the absence of any appreciable improvement in general standards of living.

In this sense there is a vicious circle for once fertility rates have started to decline

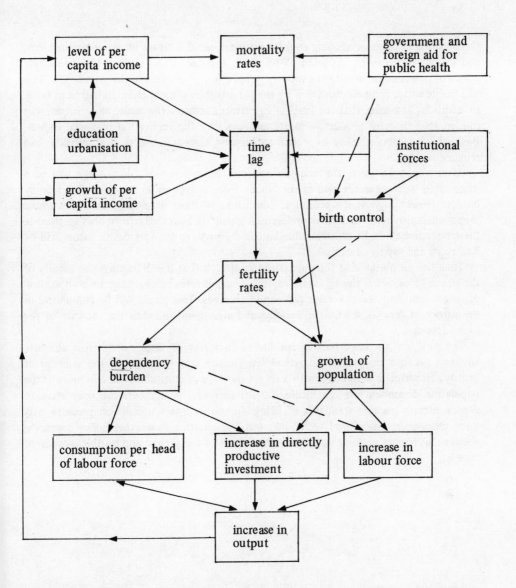

Figure 1. Flow diagram of the relationships between the growth of population and social and economic variables.

there results in most developing countries a more rapid increase in per capita incomes, and this in turn can be expected to reinforce the decline in fertility. The immediate effect of a decline in fertility is a reduced proportion of children in the population. This will enable better food consumption by the parents than if more children had been born. In addition, assuming that the level of investment remains the same, more investment can go into directly productive assets and less into the replication of social capital. Both these factors can be expected to increase output more than if fertility had remained constant.

After about 15 years the analysis becomes more complex, since there will be a more rapid increase in the size of the labour force as well as an increased dependency burden. However given the economic conditions of most developing countries where urban unemployment and rural underemployment is alarmingly high, this increase in the labour force will be mostly redundant and growth in the foreseeable future will be limited by the supply of capital.

Thus the economic case for population control is that it will improve the quality of the labour force, lower the aggragate capital - output ratio by changing the composition of investment and thereby raise per capita incomes. This effect will be cumulative as the burden of dependency falls and savings and investment rise with the increase in per capita incomes.

The analysis has been mostly conducted in terms of rates rather than absolute amounts because no precise analytical significance can be given to the concept of density. However in a country with a severe shortage of cultivable land and most of the population dependent on agriculture, further increases in numbers can only serve to depress already meagre standards of living. In the long run population pressure may force changes in agricultural techniques but the question is whether policy can bring about such changes without waiting for the impact of the ancient and terrible weapon of famine.

references and further reading

I Adelman	'An econometric analysis of population growth' *American Economic Review* June 1963
J Bourgeois-Pichat	'Population growth and development' *International Conciliation* January 1966
J C Caldwell	'Fertility attitudes in three economically contrasting regions of Ghana' *Economic Development and Cultural Change* Vol 15 No 2 January 1967
C Clark	*Population growth and land use* New York: Macmillan 1967
A J Coale	'Population and economic development' in P M Hauser ed *The population dilemma* Englewood Cliffs N J: Prentice Hall 1969
A J Coale and E M Hoover	*Population growth and economic development in low-income countries* Princeton UP 1958
D M Heer	'Economic development and fertility' *Demography* Chicago: 1969
A O Hirschman	*The strategy of economic development* New Haven: Yale UP 1958
K Krishnamurty	'Economic development and population growth in low income countries: an empirical study for India' *Economic Development and Cultural Change* Vol 15 No 1 October 1966
H Leibenstein	*Economic backwardness and economic growth* New York: Harper 1970
H Myint	*The economics of underdeveloped countries* London: Hutchinson 1965
R R Nelson	'A theory of the low-level equilibrium trap' *American Economic Review* 1956
G Ohlin	*Population control and economic development* Paris: OECD 1967
A Suavy	*The general theory of population* London: Weidenfeld and Nicolson 1969
I B Taeuber	*The population of Japan* Princeton N J: Princeton UP 1958

I B Taeuber   'Population growth in less developed countries' in
                     P M Hauser ed *'The Population Dilemma'* Prentice Hall
                     Englewood Cliffs NJ Prentice Hall: 1969

United Nations   *Growth of the world's urban and rural population 1920-
                     2000* Department of economic and social affairs, Population
                     Studies No 44 New York: 1969

United Nations   *Report on the family planning programme in India*
                     Department of economic and social affairs New York:
                     1966

United Nations   *World population prospects as assessed in 1963*
                     Department of economic and social affairs, Population
                     Studies No 41 New York: 1966

S Weintraub   'The birth rate and economic development: an empirical
                     study' *Econometrica* October 1962

chapter 3

agriculture in the development process

3.1 Introduction
In the mid 1960s economists were drawing attention to the near stagnation of food production in such populous countries as India and Pakistan and to an overall growth of food production in LDCs appreciably smaller than the combined growth of population and the demand for food from rising per capita incomes. The LDCs as a whole became net importers of food during the 1960s and famine seemed inevitable by the turn of the century.

Since 1965 there has been a dramatic increase in food production resulting from the *green revolution.* Indian food production reached an all-time record in 1968-9, and between 1967 and 1969 Pakistan increased its wheat production by 50 per cent. Such a reversal of fortune in such a short period of time should act as a salutary corrective to any tendency for dramatic generalisation. Of course as has been emphasised, population growth carries considerable momentum and the prophets of doom can claim that the increase in food production in the late 1960s only delayed the inevitable. But such arguments have been in part motivated by a desire to justify the subsidisation and over-production of European and North American agriculture, and these policies in the developed countries have in turn damaged the long-term development of agriculture in the LDCs. However before examining policy issues concerned with the prospects for the growth of the agricultural sector and reasons for its slow growth in certain countries, it is necessary to consider the role of agriculture in the development process.

3.2 The role of agriculture in development
The detrimental effects of a rapid growth of population have been shown to manifest themselves principally as a shortage of capital. However in the 1950s development economists, notably Lewis and Nurkse, saw the principal hope for poor, densely populated countries as lying in the exploitation of their surplus agricultural labour. They argued that in countries suffering from a shortage of cultivable land and with no 'labour-using' technical change, the increase in the agricultural population would be surplus to requirements. They would contribute nothing to total output, that is their marginal product would be zero, and they would exist in a state of disguised unemployment being sustained by the productive part of the population. Nurkse argued that the

agricultural output used to feed the unproductive part of the labour force could be regarded as a form of hidden savings in that if the consumption of the productive peasants remained the same while the unproductive were put to work on creating real capital, roads, irrigation works, etc a process of self-sustained growth could be initiated.

Lewis regarded the utilisation of surplus labour as a means of expanding the industrial sector, and, by increasing the productivity of labour, of creating a market which would induce further investment. In this model the demand for labour in the industrial sector is determined by the value of its marginal product. The supply of surplus labour from the agricultural sector is perfectly elastic at an institutionally determined real wage, which is sufficiently above the average product of labour in agriculture (assumed approximately equal to subsistence level) to induce labour to migrate.

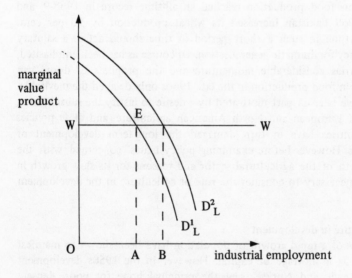

Figure 2.   The Lewis model of industrial development

Thus in figure 2, the marginal product of labour in industry is equal to D_L^1 and at a wage of OW, OA workers will be employed, producing a surplus product of WEF. It is then assumed that this surplus is invested, increasing the marginal productivity and hence demand for labour to D_L^2, at which a further AB surplus workers will be employed, and so on. Lewis recognised that this process could be terminated by an increase in the productivity of agricultural labour or by an increase in food prices relative to those of industrial goods, since both these forces would raise the institutional money wage (to keep the real wage constant) and thus reduce the surplus industrial product available for re-investment.

An analysis of such constraints has been carried out by Ranis and Fei whose important contribution is to show why investment must take place in both sectors to maintain equilibrium between the supply and demand for food and labour. Their model follows that of Lewis but they see the allocation process as falling into three phases. In the first phase, the marginal product of labour in agriculture is zero. In the second, the surplus labour has been fully utilised and thus further labour allocated to industry will have a positive marginal product but still so low as to be less than the institutional real wage. In the third phase, the marginal product of re-allocated labour is greater than the institutional wage and wages in both sectors are therefore determined by the supply and demand for labour.

Phase 2 is clearly the point where the adverse movement in the terms of trade for the industrial sector appears, since as more labour is allocated to industry so agricultural output will fall causing food prices to rise and therefore money wages in the industrial sector to rise. The rise in food prices will be accelerated in phase 3 not only because of the high marginal product of allocated labour but also because real wages in both sectors will be determined by market rather than institutional forces and hence will rise. The result of this inflation will be progressively to reduce capital formation in industry until stagnation is reached.

If the process of growth is to continue it is therefore essential that investment take place in both sectors after the point at which the surplus labour is fully utilised. The greater input of capital will extend the period of surplus labour, total output will remain constant and the food shortage of phase 2 will be postponed. At the same time, as the marginal productivity of agricultural labour is increased with the application of more capital, the point at which wages are determined by market forces is brought forward. By this process the dangerous inflationary phase 2 is eliminated and the development process proceeds smoothly from a position of exploiting its surplus labour to one where the allocation of resources is determined by market prices.

Should the economy diverge from this balanced growth path then market forces will bring it back into equilibrium. For example, if over-investment takes place in industry and under-investment in agriculture then the demand for labour will be excessively high and the supply of labour commensurately low, hence forcing up real wages and reducing industrial profits. The industrial demand for food will also be high and supply lower than would otherwise be the case thus forcing up food prices and money wages, and hence further reducing profits in the industrial sector. Industrialists will not be able to pass on the increased costs in the form of increased prices because the market for industrial goods will be correspondingly shrinking. Thus shifts in the relative profitability of the two sectors will induce investors, probably themselves landowners, to reduce investment in industry and increase it for agriculture, thus bringing the economy back onto a stable growth path.

Ranis and Fei also state that for successful development not only is a 'balanced' investment programme required but also 'labour absorbing' technical progress. In terms of the model such innovations will raise the marginal rate of substitution of labour for capital and thereby reduce the rate of decline in the marginal product of labour. In this way the industrial sector will be able to absorb a greater amount of surplus labour with a given capital stock.

It would certainly be very difficult to disagree with this prescription for the developing countries where one of the most pressing social problems is the provision of useful employment for the rapidly expanding labour force. However this prescription must be sharply distinguished from the analysis of those who conclude that the factor proportions prevailing in developing countries dictate the choice of 'labour intensive' techniques.

This argument is based on the proposition that since capital is the most scarce factor of production then output will be maximised by maximising the ratio of output to capital. If it is assumed that the opportunity cost of using labour is zero then techniques are selected which use a high ratio of labour to capital.

The weakness of this approach is that it ignores the element of time and the fact that countries have a multiplicity of goals. The implications of this are examined in chapter 6. However at a general level it can be appreciated that if it is decided to make substantial increases in standards of present consumption, then this will be at least in part at the expense of investment that would otherwise have occurred and hence may well conflict with the objective of maintaining the growth of future consumption. The choice becomes even more complex when we add the many other objectives of policy concerned with income distribution, regional balance, employment, economic independence and so on. The conclusion we should draw from this is that an economist cannot make abstract decisions about the most appropriate techniques of production or product-mix for a developing country. Such questions are directly concerned with value judgements about the interpersonal and intertemporal distribution of welfare.

The Ranis-Fei model however is open to serious criticism relating in particular to the use of the concept of *surplus labour*. Since Lewis's path breaking work this concept has come under close scrutiny and as Sen has shown, it is conceptually invalid. It is important to distinguish between open unemployment where readily identifiable people are not working at all, and the state of underemployment where everyone is working at some time in the day but where the same output could be produced by a smaller labour force working longer hours. 'Full employment' is only maintained in traditional societies by practices of work sharing. Under these circumstances it would be difficult to keep the consumption levels of those remaining on the land constant, while removing labour to the industrial sector.

One possibility would be the imposition of a land tax which forced producers to market the whole of their surplus agricultural output, but in most societies this would be impossible. An alternative would be to induce producers to sell their surplus product by diverting some of the industrial output to the production of consumer goods. What is inevitable is that the 'shortage point' will begin immediately labour is transferred and this can only be overcome by raising farm incomes, enabling them to purchase consumer goods and probably consume more of their own produce as well. The latter may of course not be wasted since by raising standards of nutrition and calorie intake it may enable farmers to work harder and longer hours thus raising the productivity of labour.

An added problem is that given the labour intensive techniques of traditional agriculture there may well be no under-employed labour, given standards of nutrition, at certain times of the year notably at sowing and harvesting. In this case, if labour is to be transferred permanently to industry these seasonal demands for labour must be removed by changing techniques of production and providing more capital. An alternative to this model of removing underemployment by providing industrial employment is to grow in a given area of land a number of crops with different seasonal demands for labour, and thus to raise agricultural productivity and incomes.

The Ranis-Fei model has thus to be considerably modified even for a 'labour-surplus' economy. It could also be argued that the problem of a food shortage only arises because of the assumption of a closed economy. As Oshima points out, countries like Ceylon, Malaya and the Philippines have constantly imported rice from Burma, Thailand, Taiwan and Vietnam. Another criticism refers to the assumption of smooth isoquants in the industrial sector, which are necessary for the steady absorption of labour with a fixed capital stock. As in the analysis of dualism it is probably more realistic to assume fixed technical inputs of labour and capital for a given output. Despite these important qualifications the model does provide a useful starting point in exploring the interdependence between the agricultural and industrial sectors and in determining what constitutes a necessary balance between these sectors.

The interdependence of agricultural production with the production of other sectors can be envisaged in the following way. Suppose there is an increase in the demand for agricultural output. To meet this demand agriculture will have to use seeds and other inputs produced by itself and in addition will require inputs from other sectors, such as chemicals, manufacturing (plant and machinery), construction (buildings, drainage, irrigation), services (financial, marketing), fuel and energy, and transportation. These demands by agriculture on other sectors constitute the backward linkages from agriculture. In addition there will be forward linkages from agriculture to the other sectors; to meet the demands of the agricultural sector, chemicals, manufacturing and so on will have to purchase some of their inputs from agriculture. To meet this further indirect demand agriculture will again have to purchase more inputs from the other sectors, and so on. Clearly the more sophisticated are techniques of agricultural production and the more developed the economy as a whole, the stronger will be the backward and forward linkages, and hence the larger will be the total demand generated from an initial increase in demand for agricultural output. The construction of tables showing such complex inter-industry flows is the concern of input-output analysis (see Robinson, chapters 1 & 2). For present purposes it is sufficient to understand the concept involved and to illustrate it as in table 7.

Table 7

Japan; Input-Output data: Demand generated per unit of final demand 1960

each unit of final demand from / induces demands in	agricul-ture	food process-ing industry	textiles	manu-factur-ing	transport and elec-tricity	construc-tion and service industries	mining
agriculture	1·241	·665	·384	·131	·033	·039	·067
food processing industry	·060	1·212	·027	·014	·004	·004	·005
textiles	·031	·027	1·623	·073	·023	·027	·020
manufacturing	·271	·402	·680	2·221	·509	·546	·350
transport and electricity	·029	·057	·079	·106	1·087	·064	·112
construction and service industries	·062	·136	·159	·167	·120	1·165	·132
mining	·015	·026	·040	·105	·069	·037	1·040
total	1·709	2·525	2·992	2·817	1·845	1·882	1·726

Source UN Economic Commission for Asia and the Far East Survey 1964

Table 7 shows the direct and indirect demands generated by a unit of final demand for the output of a particular sector of the economy. Thus if the demand for agricultural output were to increase by one thousand yen, then the output of the manufacturing sector would have to rise by two hundred and seventy-one yen, at constant prices, to meet the needs both of the agricultural sector and of the other sectors whose output is an input to agriculture. Similarly agricultural output will have to rise by two hundred and forty-one yen in addition to the increase of one thousand yen to meet the initial increase in demand. Ultimately, an initial increase in demand for the output of the agricultural sector of one thousand yen will generate a total increase in demand of over one thousand seven hundred yen. This can be contrasted with a table for India which shows that for a unit increase in demand for agricultural output, total demand increases only by 1·12.

The important point is that as agriculture develops it becomes more dependent on the output of other sectors of the economy. Admittedly this constraint can be eased by imports but there will always be a limit to the foreign exchange that is available, and for most developing countries this constraint is a very immediate one. It must also be realised that even if the supply of foreign exchange is not a constraint, many of the inputs such as marketing and financial services, the provision of power and communications and the construction of complex irrigation schemes are difficult if not impossible to import, while their domestic provision takes a considerable time and unless these gestation lags are allowed for the rate of development of agriculture will be retarded. As can be seen in table 7 the rate of agricultural development will also directly affect the rate of development of associated industries such as food processing and textiles.

To summarise, in the initial stages of development and for some considerable period thereafter the growth of the agricultural sector will be basic to the growth of national output simply on account of its sheer size in relation to other economic activities. For countries like India, Pakistan and Indonesia the share of agriculture in gross domestic product remained roughly constant at 50 per cent during the period 1953-68. Even for a rapidly developing country such as Taiwan, the proportion was still 24 per cent in 1968, against 37 per cent in 1953. Agriculture is even more important as a source of employment invariably employing 50 to 70 per cent of the labour force. Thus if agriculture grows only slowly then so too will national income and hence the size of the domestic market for industrial products. During the process of development agriculture will be of strategic importance in supplying food, labour and raw materials to the expanding industrial sector. But the process will only be sustained by increasing investment in agriculture, by which is meant not only the allocation of traditional agricultural inputs but also the diversion of a proportion of the output and services of the industrial sector to the agricultural sector. For most developing countries this necessary balance will only be marginally influenced by the ability to import since most of the scarce foreign exchange will be required to purchase imports of capital and intermediate goods to sustain the development of the industrial sector.

3.3 The relationship between inflation and agricultural production[1]

In view of the central role which the agricultural sector plays in the development process it is not surprising that a number of economists view the slow growth of per capita food production as a major cause of inflation in developing countries. Adekunle has compiled statistics on rates of inflation in 53 countries, 30 of which were LDCs, and a summary is shown in table 8.

Table 8
Rates of inflation in fifty-three countries

	1949-65	1954-9	1960-5	1965-8
		(percentage rates per annum)		
industrial countries (23)	3·7	2·35	3·41	4·1
LDCs (30)	9·89	11·99	8·03	28·6

Source Adekunle 'Rates of inflation in 53 countries' *IMF Staff Papers* 1968

It would appear that the LDCs have consistently experienced appreciably higher rates of inflation than the developed countries. However such a view would be erroneous because this result rests on the extreme behaviour of half a dozen countries, Argentina, Bolivia, Brazil, Chile, Korea and Uraguay. For example in 1959 Argentina experienced a rate of price inflation of 114 per cent and a 'normal' rate of 25 per cent per annum over the whole period since 1945. Similarly in the period studied Brazil suffered an annual rate of inflation of 60 to 80 per cent, and Chile between 30 and 40 per cent. Thus excluding these six high-inflation countries the rate of inflation of LDCs in the period 1949-68 has been between 2·7 per cent (1954-9) and 3·8 per cent (1965-8).

The suggestion that inflationary pressures may well result from food production growing at less than the required rate, which is determined by the rate of growth of population and increased demand from rising per capita incomes, has to be reconciled with the fact that food production in LDCs has indeed lagged behind demand, yet inflation has not been widespread. In addition, the predictions of neo-classical economics would entirely discount lagging food production as a cause of inflation, and indeed the whole concept of a 'required' rate of food production. In the neo-classical model a shortfall in food supplies would cause the price of food to rise, there being a low price elasticity of demand for food, real incomes would fall, expenditure on food being a large proportion of most people's incomes, causing the demand for non-food items

1 On first reading this section may be omitted.

to fall, resulting in a decrease in their price. Thus provided the supply of money was kept constant the absolute price level would be constant and the rise in food prices would be exactly offset by the fall in non-food prices. In the long run the rise in food prices and the fall in non-food prices would induce a reallocation of resources from the non-food to the food sector thus increasing food production. In a much simplified way this model approximates to the *monetarist* (IMF) view of the causes of inflation in Latin America.

The notion that lagging food production and other *structural* imperfections of supply and demand are the cause of inflation in these countries is represented in the writings of Maynard and Seers and in the publications of the Economic Commission for Latin America (ECLA), among others. The structuralists list many casual factors behind this inflation, such as prevalence of the *latifundia* (large estates), which are inefficiently managed by absentee landowners uninterested in raising agricultural productivity. Such a large low-productivity agricultural sector will have a very low price elasticity of supply of total output. To this could be added the immobility of factors of production, particularly the need for a reverse flow of labour from the urban areas. Despite large scale unemployment industrial labour will probably be strongly unionised. Considerable imperfections will exist in the goods market, such as poor communications, marketing facilities and so on, impeding the transmission of price incentives and leading to localised monopolies and monopsonies. On the demand side, given the low level of per capita incomes, derived from low productivity, a large proportion, probably 60 to 80 per cent, of incomes will be spent on a few items such as rent, clothing and food. Thus the price elasticity of demand for these items will be low, and the income elasticity of demand high.

Under these conditions, if development policies favour industrialisation to the neglect of agriculture, an excess demand for food will arise. Food prices will rise considerably on account of the high income but low price elasticity of demand, and low price elasticity of supply of food, but prices of industrial goods will fall little if at all since prices are sticky in a downward direction. Workers will resist the cut in their real wages and, being strongly unionised, will obtain higher money wages. If then it is assumed that prices depend on factor costs, particularly labour costs, and that entrepreneurs react proportionately to a fall in their profits, then a wage-price spiral results. 'Opening' the economy will not appreciably help matters because increased food imports will divert essential foreign exchange from goods required for the rest of the economy, causing stagnation. In addition agricultural exports will probably fall as some output is diverted to home consumption. Devaluation will follow, and cause further inflation.

This 'structural' analysis of inflation has been conducted in terms of the agricultural and non-agricultural sectors, but a model of structural rigidities could be applied equally to other sectors, as Seers demonstrates, such as lagging output of steel and energy, or insufficient transport facilities.

Since the structuralist model is essentially based on the underdeveloped nature of the economies and therefore appears to be an entirely reasonable analysis, why is the monetarist argument still influential in policy-making? Undoubtedly one reason is that the structuralists have been rather weak in coming forward with realistic policy solutions to deal with the immediate problem of hyper-inflation. Structural reforms by their very nature are essentially long run and will never be effected in a situation of hyper-inflation where for precautionary and speculative reasons investment will be essentially short run. A precondition for successful long-run structural reforms is some semblance of short-run stability brought about by a battery of fiscal and monetary policies, wage and price controls, credit controls and so on. It is with this in mind that Maynard and Rijcekegham describe themselves as monetarists in the short run and structuralists in the long run. This is not strictly accurate in that monetarists essentially believe that the free operation of market forces by themselves will bring about equilibrium, and the so-called structural rigidities will then disappear. For a discussion of IMF stabilisation policy in Argentina see Eshag and Thorp.

A very interesting study on lagging food supplies as a cause of inflation in eight Latin American countries for the period 1954-67 has been carried out by Edel. Edel tested two structuralist propositions: first that food production has lagged behind its required rate of growth, and secondly, that this lag is associated with inflation, balance-of-payments difficulties and stagnation. Both hypotheses were confirmed, the trend rate of growth of food production was inadequate and this was positively correlated with imports of food and negatively with agricultural exports.

Edel also shows why despite the general problem of the agricultural lag in LDCs inflation has not been widespread. In some countries such as Libya there may be a plentiful supply of foreign exchange or alternatively there may fortunately occur a favourable movement in the country's net barter terms of trade, with world food prices falling and/or the country's export prices rising. Alternatively rationing may be possible if initial consumption levels were high, or there may be the cushion of an exportable food surplus. The ability of a government to control inflation through fiscal and monetary policy and through a quick yielding agricultural programme will also be significant.

One different but related strand of the structuralist argument is that put forward by Maynard (1961) from the observation that in many LDCs agricultural exports form a large proportion of total exports (see table 9) and make a significant contribution to national income and government revenues. In addition, exports of primary products are subject in the short run to low price elasticities of supply and demand. On the supply side, because they are either minerals or plantation crops where fixed costs are a large proportion of total costs; and on the demand side because they are either foodstuffs or an industrial input which constitute a small proportion of total costs. Consequently small shifts in supply or demand conditions produce large changes in price, particularly since industrial demand for the exported commodity is a derived demand. Under boom conditions incomes and government revenues in the exporting country expand but when prices fall it is possible that all sectors will resist cuts in their income levels. Similarly it is possible that the government has committed itself to long-run development expenditures from which it cannot easily disengage itself. Excess demand will result and prices will rise.

Macbean has tested the hypothesis that LDCs are more subject to export instability than developed countries and that this is associated with inflation, but has found no evidence to support either assumption. However Maddison has criticised Macbean's methodology and maintains that by measuring fluctuations after eliminating the trend he is really measuring volatility rather than the incidence of recession. Clearly a rising trend which is occasionally retarded poses much easier policy problems, particularly from the inflation point of view, than the same volatility about a slower trend, which may thus produce on occasions an absolute decline export earnings. As is shown later primary exports are often subject to a low income elasticity of demand and hence low growth rates. In conclusion it should also be noted that Macbean's analysis was for LDCs as a whole, and thus even his own results do not exclude the possibility of individual LDCs' exports being subject to considerable instability.

3.4 Agricultural growth for the second development decade
Having surveyed the general importance of the agricultural sector in the development process it is now possible to consider some evidence on the future required growth of agriculture and the possibility of various government policies assisting the achievement of these targets. The basic objective of the Second Development Decade declared by UN in 1970 is an average annual growth of GDP for the LDCs of 6 per cent. Assuming perhaps optimistically an annual rate of growth of population of 2·5 per cent, this will result in a growth of per capita income of 3·5 per cent per annum.

On this basis the FAO (1970) estimated the required growth of the agricultural sector. An annual growth of output of 6 per cent requires that the exports of LDCs grow at a rate of rather more than 6·5 per cent. Now in 1968 agricultural products comprised on average 30·7 per cent of total export earnings and during the 1960s grew at an annual rate of 1·8 per cent. However given the low income elasticity of demand for agricultural products, and the policies of the developed countries towards importing such products (discussed further in chapter 5), it is unlikely that exports will grow by more than one per cent per year and their share in total exports by LDCs will therefore fall to 18 per cent. In addition the LDCs will have to raise their rate of growth of food production to meet the increased demand arising from a larger population and growing level of per capita incomes,[1] and to make up for the inadequate growth of food supplies in previous periods. Taking all these factors into consideration it appears that agricultural production in LDCs will have to grow by a minimum annual rate of 4 per cent. This can be contrasted with a rate of growth of just over 2 per cent in the period 1960-6.

To assist in the achievement of this target the FAO have drawn up an 'Indicative World Plan for Agricultural Development'. Thus in the Far East, cereal production will have to grow at the rate of 3·7 per cent per annum, and fruit and vegetables at 4 per cent to 4·5 per cent, to provide a better balance of diet and to meet the demand for superior foodstuffs out of increased per capita incomes. For the remaining LDCs the figures are respectively 3 per cent and just over 4 per cent.

These statistics give some idea of the magnitude of the task facing the LDCs, but it might be argued that discussing only the effective demand for food rather than the need for more food understates the problem. Unfortunately there is little agreement on this subject though it is significant that successive estimates, by both experts and alarmists, have been in a downward direction. The present range of estimates seems to lie between that of the FAO, represented by its Director of Statistics, Sukhatme, that a third of the world's population suffers from protein deficiency and that 10 to 15 per cent at any one time are lacking the necessary calories; and Clark and Haswell who claim that 'a community even at the lowest level of agricultural productivity, living predominantly on cereals, if they have enough calories will also receive enough protein'.

Part of the discrepancy between various estimates of needs lies in the difference between calories required for health (quite low) and those required for work (which for heavy manual tasks is very much higher). Requirements also depend on body size and to a lesser extent on age, sex, and climate. Even here there is a considerable conceptual problem in that the body itself adapts to low food intake by reduced weight, and through generations by changes in physical structure, and activity. Indirect evidence of a kind is supplied by the observation of deficiency diseases, though this

1 Let D be the rate of increase in the demand for food, P the rate of growth of population, η the income elasticity of demand for food, g the rate of growth of per capita income. Then $D = P + \eta g$.

may well be due to bad eating habits rather than insufficiency of food supplies.

Possibly of more significance than the total food supply of any particular country is its distribution between regions within the country and its distribution over the year. Often there are severe shortages just before harvest and a glut just after. Policies aimed at a better distribution may well have a greater impact on standards of living than simply trying to raise total output. In the latter case needs still have to be translated into effective demand in all parts of the population.

So far broad estimates of the required increase in agricultural production have been considered and these conceal large differences between countries. Thus if a country has a low level of per capita income and consequently a high income elasticity of demand for food, say 0·8, and a rate of growth of population of 3 per cent per year, then to meet the UN's target growth of per capita income of 3·5 per cent per annum, food supplies will have to grow at an annual rate of 5·8 per cent. In addition, if this country's agricultural exports comprise 50 per cent of total export earnings and total exports need to increase at the same rate as output, that is at 6·5 per cent per annum, then given the assumed rate of increase of other exports, 8 per cent, agricultural exports will have to rise by 5 per cent per annum as against the UN's maximum estimate for all LDCs of one per cent.

As may be seen in table 9, many developing countries are in a position where agricultural exports comprise substantially more than the UN average of 30 per cent of total export earnings, while in Argentina, Brazil, Ceylon, Thailand, Ghana and Uganda, the proportion is greater than 80 per cent. Thus despite a long-run tendency for the share of the agricultural sector in total exports to decline it remains, for the majority of developing countries, a very important, and in some cases crucial, source of foreign exchange earnings.

It therefore seems fairly certain that at least until 1985 agricultural output in developing countries as a whole will have to increase at an annual rate of 4 per cent, and at a proportionately higher rate if population growth exceeds an average of 2·5 per cent. For some countries with high rates of growth of population, low levels of per capita income and a high share of exports devoted to agricultural products, the agricultural sector will have to grow at an appreciably faster rate to achieve a minimum target growth of per capita incomes which is close to the average for LDCs as a whole. How plausible are these growth rates in the light of experience? Generalisations, always difficult to justify in development economics, are particularly difficult to make with regard to agricultural development, due to considerable variations in performance both between countries and within a single country over relatively short periods. For example, the maximum growth of agricultural production in any one year up to 1968 over the base years 1952-6 varies from 26 per cent for Argentina, to

Table 9
Some indicators of the economic importance of agriculture

	per cent of population in agriculture	agriculture as per cent- age of GDP	agricultural exports as a percentage of total exports
Argentina	20	15	93
Brazil	50	28	85
Colombia	50	30	76
Jamaica	44	12	40
Mexico	50	17	52
Uruguay	17	15	na
Ceylon	50	40	95
Taiwan	47	24	47
India	70	52	41
Pakistan	74	47	49
Philippines	58	32	85
Thailand	78	31	80
Turkey	73	36	88
United Arab Republic	55	28	71
Ghana	60	51	89
Kenya	84	35	58
Morocco	55	28	54
Nigeria	79	56	58
Tanzania	95	52	74
Uganda	91	58	83

Source FAO 'The state of food and agriculture 1970'

100 per cent in the case of Thailand. Variations between country performance in food production are even slightly greater. In addition to considerable variation about the trend of production of LDCs as a whole, there is also the problem of choosing the base period, which must somehow cover an average of good and bad years. Maddison (pp. 120-1) shows that while the average of agricultural output, weighted by the country's importance in total production by LDCs, grew by only 2·5 per cent per annum in the period 1949-51 to 1964-6, the unweighted average was 3·7 per cent. This difference was accounted for by the slow growth of Argentina (0·1 per cent), India (2·5 per cent) and Pakistan (1·9 per cent). It is worth noting that this average growth rate represented an appreciable acceleration both in total and per capita terms on the previous record. In addition the recent growth of agricultural output of India and Pakistan has shown substantial improvement and promises to continue for some time, natural disasters excepted.

This caveat is of course not merely routine, but a reminder that for climatic reasons developing countries also happens to be at greater risk from the extremes of floods and drought, and this combined with traditional techniques of production results in considerable fluctuation in output. Thus Thailand recorded a peak of food production in 1966, representing a 20 per cent increase on the previous year's output, while in 1967 food output fell by 14 per cent. Even greater fluctuations are recorded by Morocco.

In addition to these fluctuations in output, the trend rate of growth of *per capita* food production has tended to fall close to zero and in some cases to become negative in the past decade.

Table 10
Growth of food production per head

percentage rates per annum

	1952/4 – 1959/61	1959/61 – 1967/9
Latin America	0·3	0·1
Far East[1]	1·1	−0·1
Near East	0·8	0·3
Africa[2]	−0·2	−0·4

Source FAO, 'State of food and agriculture, 1970'
[1] excluding Japan   [2] excluding S Africa

The amount of lost ground that has to be made up between the growth of food production and that of population is further illustrated by the fact that while food production in 1968 in India, Pakistan and the Philippines represented an increase of between 40 and 60 per cent on the average production for 1952-6, this only represented a one to two per cent increase in per capita production.

On the basis of past performance an overall annual growth of agricultural output of 4 per cent seems necessary, but possibly optimistic. However as pointed out, two of the countries which depressed the average, India and Pakistan, have in recent years succeeded in increasing output substantially. In addition, as new techniques and inputs are introduced into traditional agriculture, particularly improved strains of drought resistant cereals and rice, better control over water supplies and better storage and marketing facilities, not only will total output increase but the variability of this output should fall.

The important question of course is how this can be achieved. To what extent is the output of traditional farmers responsive to price changes? What should be the role of government? Is it sufficient simply to ensure the correct internal terms of trade or should an attempt be made to change methods of cultivation by making particular inputs available, or is some comprehensive package deal required : better inputs, techniques, education, land reform, insurance etc?

3.5 The objectives of traditional farmers

The most influential study of traditional farming in recent years has been that of Schultz. His basic assumption is that traditional farmers seek to maximise individual utility in an environment of static technology, factor costs etc, and thus through a process of trial and error arrive at an optimal allocation of the resources at their disposal. The important policy conclusion arising from this analysis is that any investment which simply increased the supply of traditional factors of production would produce a very low rate of return. This theory could also be an explanation why peasant farmers, although not usually the poor of the community and having some basis for saving and investment, either do not save or place their savings in socially unproductive forms such as gold. Similarly it could partly explain the curious paradox that the labour input per acre in Japan is four times that of India. To Schultz the only source of agricultural development is to place the cultivator on an entirely different production function by 'changing the state of the arts'. By this he means a whole combination of new inputs such as mentioned above. Since this clearly cannot originate from the traditional sector, Schultz's analysis is a powerful argument for comprehensive state intervention and is in direct conflict with the *gradualist* approach of those who favour supplying particular key inputs. Schultz supports his theory by referring in particular to the studies of Hopper in India, and Sol Tax of Guatemalan Indians.

One important contribution of the study is its emphasis on the fact that because traditional farmers may be illiterate this does not mean that they are insensitive to costs and returns at the margin when allocating resources. An additional contribution is that by explaining the economic behaviour of traditional farmers in such a classical economic manner, Schultz has stimulated much useful analysis in this neglected area of development studies. A particularly constructive criticism of Schultz has been made by Lipton (1968(a)) who demonstrates that Schultz is not merely restating the tautology that peasants maximise utility, but that they maximise the marginal value product of money in each use. This is derived from Schultz's implicit assumption of a state of neo-classical perfect competition; perfect competition because otherwise individual optima would not add up to a social optimum, and neo-classical because 'no productive factors remain unemployed'.

Stated in these terms basic weaknesses appear in Schultz's argument because in many if not most developing countries nothing approximating to a perfect market in factors or goods exists. Localised monopoly and monopsony powers are widespread, particularly in land, where there is a land hunger, and products, due to poor communications and the inability of peasant farmers to store their crops, but also in labour, because of social customs. Lipton's main attack however is directed at Schultz's failure to recognise the importance of risk and uncertainty to a peasant farmer. The assumption of perfect competition entails that each farmer is able to predict with reasonable confidence the outcome of his decisions. However, given the very large variation of rainfall particularly in non-equatorial tropical and some semi-desert areas, such an assumption is invalid. Profit maximisation under these conditions is a very long-run strategy, and quite impossible as well as illogical to a peasant producer to whom the failure of his harvest represents disaster. Lipton therefore suggests that peasant farmers seek a 'survival algorithm' (a strategy which can be explicitly stated) which will guarantee them the greatest output under adverse conditions (in game theory terminology, a maxi-min solution). Since different people have different attitudes towards risk and uncertainty one would not expect the same survival strategy to be adopted by all members of a community. Furthermore in this search people will adopt various combinations of farming practices, some progressive, others less so.

In addition to its inherent plausibility this theory also explains the large differences found between farms in the same village and using the same resources. Schultz's assumption of static conditions is also curious in the light of population pressure which has not only placed an added burden on the cultivator but opened up larger urban markets. Lipton suggests that it is the attachment to an outdated survival strategy which might partly explain a low input of labour, for example, in weeding, relative to the supply of labour.

The policy conclusions resulting from the two theories of traditional agriculture are inevitably different. The Indian government in its Draft Outline of the Fourth Five Year Plan 1965 fully accepted Schultz's argument (see Lipton 1968(b)) that the 'state of the arts' must be changed and the correct assumption of a high degree of complementarity between technical inputs, fertilisers, water, improved seeds, and structural reforms, land tenure, credit systems, marketing facilities etc. Clearly this could not be applied over the whole of India, hence the decision was made to concentrate these improvements on the successful, progressive farmers who also had an assured water supply, covering about 10 to 15 per cent of the land area. Conversely, Lipton's analysis points to the possibility of increasing total output by bringing each producer up to the best cultivation standards of his neighbours.

3.6 The green revolution
The Indian situation highlights one of the possible though by no means necessary dangers of the *green revolution*[1]. By concentrating new resources on already successful farmers, already large differences in farm income will be considerably increased. In addition as output begins to expand at a significant rate, market prices will begin to fall, resulting in an economic crisis for the mass of poorer traditional farmers.

Experience of the possibilities and problems from the seed-fertiliser revolution are necessarily limited since they have only been introduced over the last four years, though their use has spread quite rapidly. The FAO estimated in 1970 that in the Far East 40 per cent, and in the Near East 8 per cent of the wheat area is planted to high yield strains, while something like 11 per cent of the rice area of the Far East is given over to these strains. In Africa and Latin America the area devoted to the new seeds is much more patchy, though particularly significant in Mexico and to a lesser extent in Brazil. It is obviously difficult to estimate the contribution of the high yield seeds to the general increase in output since weather, other inputs, and government policies could all contribute. However Willett has estimated that in the crop year 1968-9 in South and South East Asia, the contribution of high yield seeds to additional output has been about 9 per cent for rice and 20 per cent for wheat. However the provision of improved seeds on their own may only have limited effect, while all trials which have been conducted show an appreciably greater than additive effect of a package of improved seeds, plant protection, improved cultivation, fertilisers and an adequate supply of water when it is needed.

The green revolution has therefore only begun to affect yields in developing countries as a whole, but experience in Taiwan, Mexico, Philippines and the UAR shows that a considerable contribution can be made provided the correct policies are pursued. Lipton's 'survival algorithm' analysis of traditional agriculture shows that this revolution need not result in a widening inequality of the distribution of income, because the concentration of the development effort in areas of assured water supply is not the only method of raising output. If the risk and uncertainty can be reduced by giving the farmer a guaranteed minimum price for his output (minimum price because a fixed price with instability coming from the supply side would destabilise income even more than previously), and providing crop insurance for adopting innovations, then the result would be an appreciable increase in yields at low cost. Similarly the recognition that individual survival algorithms may not relate to the present, changing, situation opens up the possibility of bringing each producer

1 This means the combination of new high yielding strains of rice and cereals with sufficient fertilisers and water suppliers.

up to the best cultivation standards of his neighbour.

Johnston and Cownie point out that in the seed-fertiliser revolution we have a choice between the Mexican model, where the increase in output is concentrated in a small sector of large-scale capital-intensive farms, and the 'Japanese model' of small-scale labour-intensive and capital-saving holdings.

The immediate question raised is whether economies of scale operate with respect to size of holding. Clearly the answer to this depends on individual conditions in particular areas. They may, for instance, operate in a number of localities in Africa south of the Sahara and possibly in parts of Latin America. However, as Schultz shows, many of the indivisibilities of capital equipment are in fact only organisational problems. Where there is population pressure on the land, an assumption of constant returns to the relevant sizes of holding seems plausible. It could be argued, and some evidence in India suggests, that under these conditions where intensive cultivation is required output per acre, and hence total output, will rise as farm size diminishes. This could arise from the simple analysis shown in figure 3.

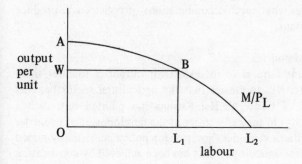

Figure 3. Relative outputs of family and commercial holdings

With land scarce relative to the supply of labour, the family plot will use labour until its marginal product is zero, producing output OA L_2. A commercial farm paying a wage OW will only employ OL$_1$ labour and produce OABL$_1$ output and the larger the farm the greater the input of wage labour. Of course it could be argued that the commercial farmer will produce a larger marketed surplus and by his greater ability to invest will maximise output in the long run.

The argument depends on the need for immediate increases in output, and on the importance of raising the marketed surplus as opposed to increasing food supplies and savings in the village. In the context of many countries, the returns from a programme which concentrates on small farmers would appear to be high. Also as Johnston and Cownie point out, large-scale capital-intensive farms will probably have to import a large part of their requirements. Conversely, Japanese technology means a large increase in demand for simple inexpensive farm equipment employing capital-saving, labour-intensive techniques of production where economies of scale are relatively unimportant and which can therefore be economically supplied from domestic resources. New high yielding varieties, by opening up the possibility of substantial increases in output relative to additional inputs of labour and capital, can be expected to induce the traditional farmer to adopt these new techniques, and to release land from cereals to produce protein foods and vegetables. A major additional advantage of the 'Japanese model' is that it will assist the agricultural sector in absorbing the inevitable future increases in the labour force for the next two or three decades until, hopefully, the growth of the labour force diminishes and the ability of the industrial sector to employ additional labour has considerably enlarged. The industrial sector itself can be expected to grow at a faster rate with the growth of the incomes of the majority of people. The important question is what specific combinations of policies will produce this form of agricultural development.

3.7 Price incentives and associated policies
One obvious incentive for peasant farmers to increase their output is to offer them a reasonable price or, more precisely, to ensure that the agricultural sector benefits from favourable internal terms of trade. As Raj Krishna has pointed out, such a policy would be a historical novelty. In the early stages of the development of countries both in the nineteenth and twentieth centuries, government policy consistently aimed at depressing the terms of trade for agriculture. This has been achieved by confiscation of part of the output, taxation, artificially depressing urban food prices to accelerate industrialisation and allowing goods purchased by farmers to rise in price. However, such policies are inappropriate in the context of the vital role which the agricultural sector must play in the development of today's developing countries, more particularly in view of past and future increases in population.

Most peasant farmers have established, in one way or another, at least some contact with product markets and hence prices influence the allocation of resources at their disposal. The question is how strongly do they react to price changes? In particular how responsive are they to changes in relative prices when deciding which combination of crops to grow? Secondly how responsive is the marketed surplus of a particular crop to a change in its price. Thirdly, how elastic is the supply of total output to changes in the terms of trade?

Work has been done on the elasticity of supply, in terms of planted acreage[1] of individual crops, to changes in relative prices rather than on the second and third relationships. Krishna quotes elasticities of 0·1 to 0·4 for changes in the prices of rice, wheat and maize relative to the price of other crops, and 0·4 to 0·7 for the commercial fibre crops of cotton and jute. For the second relationship it is possible that producers have a target size of income so that when market prices rise, the marketed surplus falls and more is consumed by the farmer. For the third relationship, elasticity may be zero because no additional resources are available to raise the total output, or negative in the case of a backward sloping supply curve. All that can be said on the latter possibility is that no one has found such adverse responses to price movements and casual empiricism suggests otherwise, but evidence of any kind is hard to come by.

Another difficulty from the planning point of view is that elasticities will certainly vary considerably between regions and possibly over a short period of time as well. Whether the objective is to encourage the adoption of the Japanese or the Mexican model, planners will also have to decide the relative importance to be given to guaranteed minimum prices or to subsidised inputs. The former policy will provide the essential guarantee against risk (for example of a price collapse due to over production), encourage the better utilisation of traditional inputs and assist planners in encouraging the desired output composition of crops. Subsidising appropriate inputs (or taxing undesirable inputs such as imported and/or capital-intensive machinery) on the other hand can encourage the adoption of the desired techniques of production to ensure that farmers only benefit to the extent that they utilise the new inputs, and avoid the possibly inflationary effects of raising food prices.

An interesting example of the operation of such policies is provided by the account of Falcon and Gotsch of how Pakistan managed during the Second Plan 1960-1 to 1964-5 to raise the agricultural growth rate from 1·2 per cent per year to 3·2 per cent, enabling the economy to grow at 5 per cent and exports at 7 per cent per annum. In a populous country like Pakistan with millions of small farms, direct public investment has at best a small effect on output. It is therefore important to provide incentives to farmers not directly affected by public investment projects. Over the years a complex and inefficient system of price controls and rationing had evolved, which not only acted as a strong disincentive to most producers but actually resulted in high and wildly fluctuating prices in food-deficit and urban areas. These controls were abandoned and the government aimed at price stability at a level

1 Not of output, because we wish to know the price responsiveness of producers when making their investment decisions. Output will depend on a variety of other conditions outside the producers' control.

sufficient to act as an incentive to farmers but avoiding inflation. Basic to this policy was the maintenance of buffer stocks, mostly wheat from the US 'PL 480' programmes, for release when prices reached a certain ceiling. Export duties on cotton and jute in which Pakistan has a comparative advantage were also reduced. Fertilisers were subsidised to bring their price to 30 per cent below world prices. (The subsidy was 50 per cent but Pakistan fertiliser plants were operating at high cost.)

The result of these price incentives was to induce an enormous private investment in tubewell irrigation in West Pakistan. By 1963-4 the annual rate of installation was 6,600 and by 1965 a total 31,500 had been installed, primarily in cotton and jute areas. Similarly fertiliser consumption doubled during the plan period. Falcon and Gotsch estimate that of the 27 per cent increase in the value of major crops grown, the contribution of the various inputs was as shown in table 11.

Table 11
Casual factors in crop production West Pakistan 1959/60 – 1964/5

	per cent
water	14
fertilisers	5
plant protection	
improved seeds	
improved cultivation	8
plus interaction effect of	
all inputs	

Source Falcon and Gotsch

Since investment in tubewells was clearly crucial, and since this movement was spearheaded by the owners of larger farms, these developments could certainly counter the argument that in conditions of 'overpopulation' a policy favouring small farms will probably maximise total agricultural output.

But conflicting evidence comes from East Pakistan where there was a significant fall in average farm size during the period 1950-60. By 1960, 50 per cent of holdings were of less than 2·5 acres. This led to an increased application of labour and an increase in cropping intensity, which was further raised by the incentive of improved terms of trade. During the plan period prices received by farmers in East Pakistan rose by 30 per cent while prices paid by them fell by 20 per cent. The result was an annual increase in rice yields of 2·1 per cent which Falcon and Gotsch attributed in the manner shown in table 12.

Table 12
Casual factors in the growth of rice production in East Pakistan 1959/60 – 1964/5

	per cent per annum
fertilisers	0·5
improved local seeds	0·5
plant protection	0·3
irrigation and drainage	0·1
labour in traditional practices	0·7
	2·1

Source Falcon and Gotsch

3.8 Land reform

Particularly important in the context of price incentives is the prevalence of share-cropping. Clearly the higher the proportion of additional output going to the landlord the greater the disincentive to the cultivator adopting any improvement. Some 'average' data for India have been calculated by Minhas and Srinivasan which clearly illustrate this point. Assumptions were made about the price received for rice and wheat output and the price of the fertiliser, while it was assumed that the cost of the fertiliser was wholly met by the cultivator, the money being borrowed at an interest rate of 10 per cent. Two different assumptions were made about variable costs: firstly, that they represented 10 per cent of the output price: and secondly, 20 per cent. Finally, three assumptions were made about tenure: complete ownership, 50 per cent of the output, and finally 40 per cent. The results were as follows:

Table 13
Returns to the use of fertilisers under share-cropping

Crop	cultivator's share	optimal dosage of nitrogen (kgs/ha) given that variable cost is		net revenue/ha given that variable cost is		net returns as % of fertilisers' cost given that variable cost is	
		10%	20%	10%	20%	10%	20%
new variety of wheat	100%	88·4	84·9	256·5	210·4	159	136
	50%	60·5	53·6	60·3	42·0	107	89
	40%	46·6	37·9	28·6	16·9	34	24
existing variety of wheat irrigated	100%	47·0	45·6	207·9	149·7	242	180
	50%	35·7	32·9	65·2	60·1	79	65
	40%	30·1	26·5	29·3	20·3	53	42
existing variety of wheat unirrigated	100%	32·6	30·2	49·8	37·9	84	69
	50%	13·3	8·2	4·0	1·0	17	7
	40%	3·3	–	0·2	–	3	–

Table 13 (cont'd.)

Crop	cultivator's share	optimal dosage of nitrogen (kgs/ha) given that variable cost is		net revenue/ha given that variable cost is		net returns as % of fertilisers' cost given that variable cost is	
		10%	20%	10%	20%	10%	20%
rice	100%	43·2	41·8	167·9	139·3	213	183
	50%	33·1	30·3	49·2	36·9	81	67
	40%	28·0	24·6	28·2	19·3	55	43

Source Minhas and Srinivasan

In the case of existing varieties of unirrigated wheat, the net return on the use of the fertiliser, with variable costs equal to 20 per cent and with the cultivator deriving the whole of the benefit, was 69 per cent. But with 50 per cent share-cropping, the return to the farmer fell to a meagre 7 per cent. However, it is worth noting that in the case of improved high yield wheat under the same cost conditions, the return on 50 per cent share-cropping was 89 per cent.

It is also worth remembering that share-cropping benefits the tenant because it is a partial insurance against crop failure, therefore if planners wish to abolish it they must replace it by an equally effective insurance.

Land reform, in addition to providing some regulation of rents, may also aim to provide security of tenure and a more equitable distribution of land. Probably the easiest and most effective method of achieving rent control and providing security of tenure is by giving the 'land to the tiller'. Since this is the least dislocative method of reform and since it identifies output more closely with ownership, it happily marries the economic objective of maximising output, at least in the short run, with political expediency. In India, 78 per cent of the farmland is wholly cultivated by the owners (Lipton). Redistribution of land above a certain ceiling to those with very small holdings, to the landless, or to form cooperatives seems to have had very limited success in most countries and as table 14 shows inequalities in the distribution of land seem to be quite prevalent.

In India 14 per cent of holdings cover 60 per cent of the acreage while 60 per cent of holdings are of less than 5 acres. On the basis of the economic analysis of traditional agriculture, a better distribution would probably raise total output, but as Thorner shows, the landowners are inevitably the ones with political power.

Probably the most productive land reform has been the consolidation of holdings which have become fragmented over generations due to laws of inheritance and, in recent years, the increase in population. The consolidation of plots of land is certainly an example of increasing returns to all factor inputs, if only in the saving of time wasted in travelling from one plot to another.

Table 14
Distribution of land in selected Asian countries

	per cent of holdings less than 5 acres	per cent of total acreage
Ceylon	85	30
W Pakistan and Philippines	80	45
E Pakistan	77	43
W Malaysia	66	45

Source UN Economic Commission for Asia and the Far East, Survey 1970

Land reform in Africa south of the Sahara, in addition to dealing with the problem of fragmentation of land, has fundamentally had to find a solution to the breakdown of systems of communal land tenure and shifting agriculture based on 'slash and burn'. Briefly, the traditional system was based on cutting down and burning the vegetative cover thus transforming the plant nutrients into ash which is added to the soil. This was then followed by shallow cultivation. The fertility of the soils however is often confined to a shallow surface layer and the removal of the protective layer of vegetation exposes the soil to leaching and erosion caused by the heavy tropical rains. The fertility of the soil falls to such a level that the land must be abandoned and soil fertility allowed to build up again. This restorative period varies widely from being about zero on the rich alluvial soils of the Niger and Zambesi to a period of about 10 years in most of W. Africa and up to 20 years for south central Africa.

Under this system the maximum density of population which the land can support is fairly low. The stability of this system has been shattered by the rapid introduction of cash crops, such as coffee in East Africa and cocoa in Ghana, which have taken up large areas of land previously available for migration, and by the rapid growth of population. As Clark and Haswell demonstrate, these pressures have been accentuated by the fact that the distribution of population bears a low correspondence to the distribution of fertile soils. Under these conditions the system of communal land tenure has had to be abandoned despite its advantage as a system of social security. Clearly a fundamental change in techniques of production was required with more intensive cultivation, though this varies widely depending on the area, and above all on investment in the land in soil improvement and water supplies, improvement of cattle stocks and other forms of long-term investment. This will only be achieved if the farmer has security of tenure and the ability to enclose his land. Fortunately the customary system often has many of the essential features of the freehold system and the transition has been, and probably will be, not too difficult.

The most advanced developments along these lines have taken place in Kenya, particularly since the Swynnerton plan of 1954. The objective was to bring traditional farmers into greater contact with the market and hence raise their standard of living by encouraging the growing of cash crops, particularly coffee. Thus while cash crops comprised only 9 per cent of the value of smallholder production in 1954, the proportion had increased by 1964 to 36 per cent. A prerequisite for this development was the consolidation and enclosure of holdings and the granting of individual title, and by 1965 three million acres in the former reserves had been consolidated or enclosed, leaving a further five and a half million acres of high-potential land to be consolidated. As in the case of India, care will have to be taken that, in the drive to raise the marketed surplus, the mass of subsistence farmers are not left far behind.

3.9 Credit

It has been emphasised that there is probably scope for low-cost methods of increasing agricultural output, but that the cultivator will probably have to engage in some expenditure. An essential complement to government farm expenditure is therefore the provision of credit for the purchase of additional inputs. Theoretically, credits should be closely related to the costs and benefits derived from the additional inputs, and from this point of view the linking of agricultural banks with the extension service can prove valuable. However to some extent this is a 'western' approach divorced from the reality of peasant agriculture, where consumption and investment decisions are closely related. Indeed Thorner shows that one of the major reasons why some Indian credit cooperatives have failed to break the hold of the local moneylender is that the former give credit only for farm inputs and insist on payment once the crop is sold while the moneylender will lend for all purposes and for long periods, though of course at very high interest rates. Basically then the need is often for long-term loans.

A fundamental requirement for the success of all these policies, price incentives, marketing facilities, the supply of new or additional inputs, credit facilities, extention service, education, land consolidation and so on, is the provision of an adequate low-cost transport system. For example, the cost of any input to the farmer is its factory price plus the cost of transport. The price he receives for his output is the central market price minus the cost of transport. Similarly the cost of providing an adequate extension service may be prohibitively high where poor communications exist. This is perhaps the closest example of the Nurkse hypothesis of using 'surplus labour' (off-peak) for capital formation in a project with large and immediate returns to all concerned. Its provision is also a necessary pre-conditon for the establishment of viable agro-industries to provide employment for the increase in the labour force which cannot be absorbed by agriculture.

3.10 Agriculture as a source of savings

Although peasant farmers have low levels of per capita income, they are by no means the poor of the agricultural community, and as incomes rise with low-cost labour-intensive techniques of production so will the potential excess of rural saving over rural investment. As Ohkawa has shown for Japan in the late nineteenth and early twentieth centuries, agricultural savings were 12 per cent of agricultural incomes and since only a quarter of these savings had to be invested, this left a steady 9 per cent of agricultural incomes available for non-agricultural investment. Since the rate of non-agricultural investment was 21 per cent and of non-agricultural savings was 14 per cent, agricultural savings financed a third of non-agricultural investment. Similarly in Taiwan the agricultural sector provided a third of national income during the period 1952-62 but provided 40 per cent of domestic savings.

However, as was previously mentioned, there has been a tendency in some countries to carry forced savings to extremes by adversely moving the internal terms of trade by the use of marketing boards, and to a lesser extent by taxing the sale of farm output. The result in some cases has been a slow growth of output and possibly an even slower growth of the marketed surplus as farmers retreated back into the subsistence sector. One solution to these excesses could be a progressive tax on the size of holding, and little or none on output. In addition to raising revenues this would also encourage the splitting up of large estates, where this is desirable, and would not act as a disincentive to progressive farmers increasing their output. However further discussion on this and other taxation issues takes us into an analysis of the finance development.

3.11 Summary

In discussing the role of agriculture in the development process the need for 'balance' between agricultural and industrial development has been emphasised. This need for a balanced relationship arises from the following considerations.

The agricultural sector will provide industry with its supply of labour. Too high a level of real incomes in the industrial sector relative to agriculture will cause an excess supply of industrial labour, resulting in urban unemployment and agricultural stagnation. This in turn will cause considerable inflation and a consequent retardation of the growth of the economy.

It is important to recognise that, since up to 80 per cent of the population live in the agricultural sector, income levels here will basically determine the market for industrial goods. In this way, neglect of agricultural development will soon bring to a standstill any attempt at forced industrialisation.

The introduction of foreign trade into the model will in the case of most countries do little to modify these conclusions. Food deficiencies can certainly be met by imports, but foreign exchange is almost certainly in short supply. To the extent to which imports have to be paid for in the currency of the developed countries, this will mean less foreign exchange available to purchase the imports required to sustain the industrialisation programme. Similarly there would appear to be little immediate possibility of many countries accelerating development through concentrating on manufactured goods for export. Most of these goods would have to be exported to the developed countries and, as is discussed in chapter 4, the latter have considerable tariff and non-tariff barriers in precisely those markets in which the LDCs are potentially competitive. In addition, the manufacturing industries in LDCs will probably not be initially competitive in world markets due to the need to acquire skills and economies of scale. Thus the argument returns to the proposition that in the initial stages the industrial sector will probably be heavily dependent on the growth of a protected home market.

Indeed 'opening' the economy emphasises, rather than reduces, the importance of agricultural development. This is particularly evident where agriculture makes a significant, and in some cases a dominant, contribution to export earnings. Foreign exchange earnings in turn are often the major limitation on development.

As development proceeds, additional links will develop between the two sectors. More sophisticated agricultural techniques will increasingly impose demands on the industrial sector and, to a lesser extent, part of the inputs of industry will be derived from agriculture.

Considerations such as these led to the conclusion that, if LDCs as a whole are to grow at an annual rate of 3·5 per cent per capita in the period 1970-80, then the agricultural sector will have to expand by 4 per cent per annum. For a number of countries this expansion will have to be appreciably greater than 4 per cent.

The fundamental question is how this can best be achieved. Is it possible to relay on a large 'package deal' programme of new seeds, fertilisers, adequate water supply, better techniques, good marketing facilities etc? The considerable cost of this package would necessitate concentration on the most successful farmers. An alternative programme is to raise the standards of the majority of farmers up to the cultivation practices of the successful farmers. This crucial question was discussed by contrasting Schultz's analysis of traditional agriculture with that of Lipton, and it was concluded that there was probably considerable scope for low-cost methods of raising agricultural productivity. Emphasising the possibility of raising output by improving the practices of the less efficient does not however preclude a limited 'package deal' programme for for most efficient.

The social results of the policies are also important. Exclusive support to the most efficient farmers will widen the considerable existing gap in standards of living between farmers. Similar considerations arise in the discussion by Johnston and Cownie of the choice between the Mexican model and the Japanese model in the context of the green revolution.

Clearly the provision by governments of the inputs necessary to accelerate agricultural development will not be sufficient in anything but a command economy. Incentives will be equally, if not more, important. By the term incentives is meant a complex bundle comprising the internal terms of trade, the institutional arrangements governing land holdings, and marketing and distributional facilities. The relative importance of these factors will obviously depend on the country being considered. However, the study of Pakistan demonstrated that the combination of favourable internal terms of trade, combined with an insurance scheme against price collapse, can produce quite spectacular results. In another country the lack of security of tenure or high share-cropped rents may be a crucial disincentive to the adoption of new techniques or to working the land more intensively.

Finally, given the low level of incomes of the majority of cultivators, the supply of credit will probably be crucial in enabling farmers to purchase improved inputs. However, the attempt to confine the use of this credit to a narrow definition of 'investment' as opposed to 'consumption' will probably not be very useful in the context of traditional agriculture where consumption standards are already low for much of the year.

references and further reading

J O Adekunle   'Rates of inflation in fifty-three countries' *IMF staff papers* 1968

C Clark and Mr Haswell   *The economics of subsistence agriculture* London: Macmillan 1967

M Edel   *Food supplies and inflation in Latin America* New York: Praeger 1969

E Eshag and R Thorp   'The economic and social consequences of orthodox economic policies in Argentina' *Bulletin of the Oxford Institute of Economics and Statistics* 1965

W F Falcon and C H Gotsch   'Lessons in agricultural development' in G F Papanek (ed) *'Development policy: theory and practice'* Harvard UP 1968

B F Johnston and J Cownie   'The seed-fertiliser revolution and the labour force absorption problem' *American Economic Review* 1969

Raj Krishna   'Agricultural price policy and economic development' in B F Johnston and H Southworth (ed) *Agricultural development and economic growth* Cornell UP 1967

W A Lewis   'Economic development with unlimited supplies of labour' *Manchester school of economic and social studies* 1954

M Lipton   'The theory of the optimising peasant' *Journal of Development Studies* 1968 (a)

M Lipton   'Strategy for agriculture urban bias and rural planning' in P Streeten and M Lipton (ed) *The crisis of Indian planning* Oxford UP 1968

A Macbean   *Export instability and economic development* London: Allen and Unwin 1966

A Maddison   *Economic progress and policy in developing countries* London: Allen and Unwin 1970

G Maynard   'Inflation and growth on Latin America' *Oxford Economic Papers* 1961

G Maynard   *Economic development and the price level* London: Macmillan 1961

G Maynard and W Rijeckeghem	'Stabilisation policy in an inflationary economy' in G Papanek (ed) *Development policy : theory and practice* Cambridge Mass: Harvard UP 1968
B S Minhas and T N Srinivasan	'New agricultural production strategy' in A M Khurso (ed) *Readings in agricultural development* Bombay: Allied Publishers 1968
R Nurkse	*Problems of capital formation in underdeveloped countries* Oxford: Blackwell 1953
K Ohkawa	'The role of savings in Japanese economic development' in *Economic Commission for Asia and Far East Survey* UN 1964
H Oshima	'Comment on the Ranis-Fei model' in Eicher and Witt (ed) *Agriculture in economic development* New York: McGraw Hill 1964
G Ranis and J C Fei	'A theory of economic development' *American Economic Review* 1961
G Ranis and J C Fei	*Development of the labour surplus economy: theory and policy* Homewood Ill: Richard D Irwin Inc. 1964
P Reddaway	*The development of the Indian economy* London: Allen and Unwin 1962
J N Robinson	*Planning and forecasting techniques* London: Weidenfeld and Nicolson 1972
T W Schultz	*Transforming traditional agriculture* Yale UP 1964
E F Schumacher	'Industrialisation through intermediate technology' in R Robinson (ed) *Industrialisation in developing countries* Cambridge: UP 1965
D Seers	'A theory of inflation and growth' *Oxford Economic Papers* 1963
A K Sen	*Choice of techniques* Oxford: Blackwell, 1960
P V Sukhatme	'The world's food supplies' *Journal of the Royal Statistical Society* 1966
D Thorner	*Agricultural co-operatives in India,* New York: Asia Publishing House 1964
UN	*Indicative world plan for agricultural development* FAO (provisional, 1969)
UN	*The state of food and agriculture* FAO 1970

UN

Towards accelerating development - proposals for the second development decade New York: Department of economic and social affairs 1970

J W Willett

'Impact of new varieties of rice and wheat in Asia' Washington: *AID Spring Review* 1969

chapter 4

the finance of development

4.1 Introduction

Given a target rate of growth of GDP in developing countries of 6 per cent per annum, and a capital-output ratio of between 3:1 and 4:1, the required rate of capital formation is between 18 and 24 per cent of GDP. The figures are purely illustrative, since the use of the capital-output ratio is subject to very considerable conceptual and practical difficulties, but they give some idea of the magnitude of the task facing the developing countries. Of course, if a country has a rich natural resource base of petroleum or minerals then by exchanging these resources for the output of other countries a high level of capital formation can be sustained. Alternatively, assistance may come from other countries by way of aid or private investment. However, for the majority of developing countries most of the resources for capital formation will have to come either directly from the domestic economy, or by transforming domestic resources into exports and thereby obtaining capital and intermediate products. Table 15 gives some figures on these relationships.

Table 15
Investment and external sources of finance 1963-67

	gross fixed investment as a percentage of GDP 1963-7	external finance as a percentage of GDP 1963-7	percentage growth of GDP 1960-8
Argentina	16–20	−1·8 to −0·2	2·9
Brazil	11–16	−1·7 to +1·3	4·7
Chile	16	+1·1 to +4·5	4·5
Columbia	16–18	+1·4 to +4·5	4·5
India	15–16	+2·3 to +2·66	4·0
Philippines	17–20	+1·9 to +3·5	5·7
Taiwan	14–18	−0·2 to +3·54	10·1

Source Column 1 and 3 UN statistical yearbook; Column 2 Maddison Table D-3 (shows external finance in a national accounting sense only) − = net outward flow

As Maddison shows (p.55), external finance, with the exception of a few countries like Taiwan, Israel and Greece, has been a relatively minor source of resources since

1950 and in addition has been relatively unstable over short periods. The UN World *economic survey* for 1965 (part I) produced a study on savings in LDCs and from this it would appear that the volume of savings has been 'generally inadequate in relation to most growth objectives'. There were of course wide inter-country differences in performance, but the median value of domestic savings for the period 1962-4 was 13 per cent of GDP, compared to 20 per cent in the developed countries. This discrepancy in savings rates can of course be explained by the 'vicious-circle' argument that the propensity to save increases as income rises but income will only rise if there is a prior increase in savings and investment. As with most vicious-circle arguments it is not a particularly useful analysis because it fails to explain why some countries have managed to save much more than others out of a given level of per capita income.

Specifically, LDCs are not only characterised by a low level of per capita income but by a very marked concentration of the income in a small section of the population. On this basis it is possible that the savings base for LDCs would not be materially different from that of developed countries. Indeed it was by such a mechanism that today's rich countries became developed. Unfortunately the privileged few in today's developing countries appear either to have a high propensity to consume (which Nurkse explains by the international demonstration effect of developed countries' consumption standards), or alternatively to invest overseas in the developed countries.

In this situation governments must play a decisive part in raising the rate of domestic savings and investment. They can in principle induce the desired transfers of resources by discouraging undesirable economic behaviour in the private sector, by using fiscal and monetary policy and by allowing the public sector to become appreciably larger than in developed countries. However as the UN report shows the reverse is the case, for the share of government in GDP averages about 15 per cent in LDCs and in many cases is less than 12 per cent, while in developed countries it is seldom less than 25 per cent. From the evidence available it seems clear that this discrepancy is directly due to the failure of government revenues to keep pace with the increase in consumption expenditure.

One theoretical possibility is for the government to finance development by inflation. As prices rise, income is distributed towards profit earners who, having higher levels of income, tend to save more. In addition, with prices rising and government securities carrying a fixed rate of interest, the real cost of servicing the national debt will be reduced. However, as Maynard demonstrates, in the realistic situation of LDCs, where the marginal propensity to consume of profit-earners is not substantially different from the average propensity of the whole community and where the wage-price coefficient is close to unity, then even a small increase in investment can only be financed at a ridiculously high rate of inflation. Similarly, as Rao shows, deficit financing will increase only money incomes and not real incomes, given the high income, low price-elasticity of demand for food, and the low (at least in the short run) price-elasticity of supply of this principal wage good. Governments therefore have little option but to try to improve the basis of their tax revenues.

4.2 The structure of government revenues

One immediately obvious feature of government revenues in LDCs is the heavy reliance on indirect taxes, typically accounting for 60 to 70 per cent of revenues, compared with a proportion of about 40 per cent in the UK. Conversely, income assessed for personal taxation comprises about 75 per cent of GNP in the UK and only 5 per cent in Africa. Given the relative levels of development there is of course nothing necessarily wrong with this situation. If income tax is to be anything more sophisticated than a poll tax, individual income and expenditure must be assessed. In a country with considerable illiteracy, where few people maintain adequate accounts of transactions, where the requisite administrative abilities are in very short supply and where per capita income is low, a comprehensive system of income tax would be worse than useless.

However, granted this, it is still argued, for example by Prest, that governments in LDCs have failed to develop an equivalent yield on their income tax to that of developed countries because they have failed to apply the appropriate rate of tax. This has often arisen because they have fashioned their tax system on the model of a developed country and applied the same rate of tax to the same absolute, instead of relative, income level. For example in an LDC the rate of tax on 15,000 units of income, equivalent to £1,500 pa in the UK, may be the same as that in the UK, but 15,000 units may be 40 times the income of the poorest worker in that country whereas in the UK £1,500 pa is only about double that of the poorest paid. Thus the wealthy individual in the LDC is relatively very lightly taxed. A similar point is made by Kaldor when he says that the problem in LDCs is not so much their low taxation potential as the low coefficient of utilisation of this potential. The tax base is adequate because of the heavily skewed income distribution at the upper end of the scale and, since this is closely associated with the ownership of land in countries with a serious shortage of cultivable land, he advocates a tax on the value of produce per acre. One objection is that if Kaldor's analysis is correct the incidence of the tax would presumably fall on the cultivator not the landowner, and would therefore be inequatable. Secondly, on the basis of the analysis in chapter 3, a fixed tax based on potential yield would appear superior to a variable one based on output, for the latter could have a strong disincentive effect. However Kaldor's analysis of taxable potential would still appear to be valid.

Possibilities for increased revenues from income tax may therefore exist in many developing countries but fundamentally the increase in revenues must come from indirect taxation. The UN study found that between 15 and 40 per cent of total tax revenues came from import taxes with a generally much smaller proportion coming from exports. Table 16 gives some examples of the components of government revenues in 1953-5 and 1962-4.

Table 16
Components of central government revenue 1953/5 and 1962/4

percentage of total revenue

	year	taxes on income and wealth	taxes on foreign trade of which:			taxes on internal trans- actions	other
			total	import taxes	export taxes		
		1	2	2a	2b	3	4
Ecuador	I	12	46	40	7	34	8
	II	14	52	39	13	22	13
Burma	I	22	25			12	42
	II	28	26			26	20
Ghana	I	11	73	31	33	2	15
	II	16	57	37	14	13	14
Philippines	I	16	33	33	–	37	13
	II	22	23	23	–	41	13
India	I	19	25	20	5	23	32
	II	22	17	16	–	32	30

Source UN World economic survey 1965
Note I = 1953-5 II = 1962-4

A tax on foreign trade is justifiable both on the grounds of its importance relative to national income and its relative ease of administration. The major disadvantages are that it may well be on a shrinking base, and that it is subject to considerable fluctuations over a short period. The latter instability arises because during an exported boom this source of revenue will increase and, in addition, as incomes rise so will imports given the usually high marginal propensity to import, and thus government revenues will expand considerably. But once income growth slows down or even falls then the growth of tax revenue will decline as imports fall. This source of revenue will also be on a shrinking base if the economy is moving into a period in which growth is constrained by shortage of foreign exchange. This could arise from a structural problem of transforming domestic resources into foreign exchange. In this situation imports will be limited to goods and services which are essential to the development effort and thus can only be lightly taxed if inflation and the retardation of growth are to be avoided. Penal import duties will be placed on non-essentials, but this will be specifically for the purpose of limiting their entry.

Thus regrettably governments are forced to place taxes on goods of mass consumption, although there would appear to be some confusion on what exactly this implies. Chelliah (pp.85 – 90) demonstrates the confusion that can arise when a purely revenue-allocation, as opposed to resource-allocation, point of view taken on this issue. The role of a tax on mass consumption goods is not to raise the rate of investment at any given time, and hence depress already low levels of consumption, but to restrict the *growth* of consumption out of rising income levels. The taxation of the increase in the per capita output of these essential commodities will not affect present consumption or output, and resources will not be released from these sectors. However, such a tax on marginal additions to the output of mass consumption goods will discourage further investment in these sectors and thus release future resources for capital formation. In addition, high rates of tax must be placed on non-essential goods with a high income elasticity of demand, thereby ensuring the desired use of future resources.

An additional attraction in taxing non-essentials rather than goods of mass consumption is that it meets the criteria of equity, since the basket of goods comprising middle and upper-class consumption is often entirely different from that of mass consumption. These goods will probably have a low price elasticity of demand and hence ensure the maximum diversion of resources from the private to the public sector by those most able to afford this forced saving. From the point of view of diverting resources from particular industries, we can say that the greater the elasticity in the supply and demand curves over the relevant price range the greater the resource allocation effect of a commodity tax. This is illustrated in figure 4 where A shows the contrasting effects of price elastic and relatively inelastic supply, and B shows the effects of elastic and inelastic demand.

In the price inelastic cases the resources allocated are represented by the fall in output from Q_1 to Q_2 and in the price elastic cases by the greater fall in output from Q_1 to Q_3.

The need for a general resource allocation point of view on the levying of taxes is underlined by the experience of countries which have imposed high import duties on non-essentials but not on the domestic consumption of these goods. The inevitable

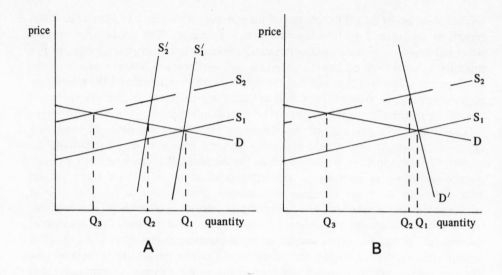

Figure 4. Resource allocation effect of a commodity tax

result was the diversion of domestic investment towards import substitution of these goods. If domestic value-added was low in these lines of production, then the purpose of the import duty, to save foreign exchange, was mostly thwarted. Even if domestic value added was high, it still implied either the diversion of resources from goods which would have been exported, or from development oriented investment projects. There is, therefore, a strong case on resource allocation grounds for levying a general tax on domestic production as well as imports of goods whose consumption has to be discouraged.

A further resource allocation problem may arise if for political and social reasons it is not feasible to tax foodstuffs. As Little points out, the tax structure must be planned in such a way that it preserves a balance between the supply and demand for food and non-food items independently. This is essential because there will be little possibility of allocating resources used for non-food production to increase food production in the short run, yet if non-food products are heavily taxed, people may well switch some of their expenditure towards an increased demand for food. Thus, given the price elasticities of demand for food and non-food goods, the system of indirect taxes must have a neutral effect on the consumption of these items. This will be achieved by estimating the substitution effect of the tax and ensuring that agricultural output expands sufficiently to meet this increased demand as well as the demand from other sources.

A number of ingenious proposals have been tried in developing countries, notably the use by India of Kaldor's expenditure tax (Chelliah pp 172-4), while Higgins (chapter 25) has put forward an intriguing basis for a self-enforcing tax system. However it appears that considerable advances could be made in raising the ratio of savings to national income and in improving the allocation of resources, by building on and improving, as well as simplifying, the existing tax structures of LDCs, and by charging the full economic cost of providing many public services. As pointed out already, most of the resources for accelerating development will inevitably have to come from the LDCs themselves, although an increased quantity as well as a better quality of financial flows may come from the developed countries.

4.3 Private foreign capital in developing countries

Private investment in developing countries is synonymous in the minds of many people with exploitation of these countries. Certainly in the nineteenth century, some of the direct investment in mines and plantations contributed little or nothing to the development of the country, and indeed a strong case could be put forward to show that it was detrimental to their development. However even in this era, it must be remembered that until the 1930s the bulk of overseas investment was bilateral portfolio investment, providing finance to national and local authorities and large corporations, for the construction of social overhead capital. The important point to remember is that historical precedent is of no value when analysing the value of present foreign investment in developing countries, for the composition of this investment is radically different.

In 1970 bilateral portfolio investment comprised only 20 per cent of the total flow of $4·6 billion of long term capital to developing countries, while direct investment comprised 75 per cent, the remaining 5 per cent comprised portfolio investment with international agencies such as the World bank.

In recent years the US has provided just under half the net flow of direct investment in developing countries with UK, Germany, France and Japan providing another third. Such investment is commonly associated with investment in petroleum and mining and certainly just over 40 per cent of both the total stock of private foreign investment in LDCs in 1967 and the flow of investment in 1965-70 were in these sectors. However some 30 per cent of the stock of foreign investment in 1967 and 37 per cent of the flow in 1965-70 was in the manufacturing sector of developing countries, and it is in this sector that the important dynamic benefits of foreign investment, associated with the transfer of technology and skills and 'linkage' effects, will be mostly concentrated.

It is therefore a matter of concern that the bulk of foreign investment, particularly new manufacturing investment, is concentrated in Latin America, mostly in Argentina, Colombia and Mexico. Conversely, South and South-East Asia have received relatively little direct investment. In other words most foreign investment goes to developing countries with relatively higher levels of per capita income, attracted by the larger size of market and better facilities for conducting an enterprise. This is of course what one would expect to occur under the operation of market forces, and it suggests important implications for the current debate on whether developing countries would benefit from more foreign investment rather than more official bilateral aid. In particular, while LDCs with relatively high standards of living might well attract more private investment, the poorer countries with the majority of the population of the developing world will continue to rely heavily on official aid for the foreseeable future.

A recent study by Dunning and Pearce shows that not only is private investment in developing countries heavily concentrated among the few relatively better-off countries but the share of LDCs in overseas investment, particularly manufacturing investment, is declining. The most obvious explanation, that investment in LDC's produces a lower rate of return, is according to Reddaway incorrect. It might be argued that the restrictions placed on foreign investment by developing countries, such as confining it to approved industries, the insistence on the employment of a strictly limited number of foreign personnel, the control of the repatriation of profits, capital and individual earnings and so on, are all barriers to increasing foreign investment. On the other hand, in these countries, the free operation of market forces will probably lead to a slower rate of development. (See chapter 6.) A clearly stated investment code, directly integrated with a good development plan, will produce a much more dependable environment for evaluating both opportunities and risks.

An unfavourable climate for foreign investment is usually derived not from the existence of controls but from the lack of an explicit and well formulated set of restrictions. In recent years the LDCs have established a whole battery of tax incentives, ranging from relief of duties on imports, to relief from income tax, sometimes at appreciable cost to themselves in terms of lost governmental revenues. At best, such incentives appear to be of minor importance in attracting foreign capital, and unless the effects of such incentives are carefully calculated beforehand they may lead to undesirable forms of investment. For instance, the remittance of duties on imported capital goods, if successful, will attract capital-intensive industries which will contribute little in providing local employment, and encouraging the growth of local ancillary industries. Similarly, tax holidays consisting of the partial or complete exemption from income tax for an initial specified period may simply attract quick yielding forms of investment contributing little to the development effort. Possibly of more use is the practice of a number of governments in the developed countries of providing investment insurance against political risks, such as expropriation, for their nationals for a period of years.

Despite these disturbing aspects of the spread of private investment to developing countries, foreign private investment clearly has an important part to play in assisting the progress of developing countries. However this brief discussion of some of the incentives which LDCs offer to foreign investors illustrates the fact that we lack any systematic criteria by which its usefulness can be evaluated.

The particular value of foreign investment must lie in providing resources which would not otherwise have been available. This may take the form of a technology, skills and access to markets which could not be obtained at lower cost by alternative means. The alternative, for example, may be a licensing agreement whereby the owner of the patent in a developed country grants a company in an LDC the right to manufacture, in return for financial compensation. It is possible, however, that the terms of the licensing agreement may be too costly or restrictive, for example forbidding export, or the developing country may not have sufficient technical and managerial knowledge and skill to use the process and may be unable to hire foreign personnel to fill this gap.

When assessing the contribution of a particular form of foreign investment one would also like to ask to what extent there would have been a demand for the product in the absence of the foreign company, and whether in fact most of the demand was created by their skill in advertising. In practice this will be extremely difficult to judge while, in addition, one must also ask what would have been purchased in the absence of this product.

An important question concerns the ability of such investment to achieve a large and sustained transfer of foreign exchange resources to the developing country. The answer to this is quite complex for, although an initial transfer of capital to establish the enterprise will be favourable, this may be quickly offset by the purchase of most of the inputs, including labour, from the investing country and by the repatriation of most of the profits, with little local-reinvestment. Indeed the direct balance of payments effect may be negative from the beginning if the initial capital is raised in the developing country and most of the inputs are purchased abroad. This, however, is only part of the analysis since the product may have been produced in any case by an indigenous producer, or alternatively may have been imported. Clearly foreign investment is potentially more beneficial in the latter case.

It is also necessary to determine the opportunity cost of the indigenous resources utilised by the foreign enterprise. If this is assumed to be zero then clearly a very wide range of projects will be potentially beneficial to the economy. However, as was discussed in chapter 3, this will rarely be the case and one must therefore ask what would have been the direct and indirect contribution to the balance of payments of the alternative use of these resources. In other words, it is necessary to estimate the social marginal product of the private investment against the alternative, if any, that it displaces. If the investment is making the greatest possible contribution to national output, it will also lead to an improvement in the balance of payments.

An interesting analysis of the effect of foreign private investment on the balance of payments and national income of small developing countries is that by Needleman and associates of Jamaica and Kenya. Given the resources and information available to them, the authors concentrated on the effect of *marginal* changes in foreign investment and did not attempt to evaluate the likely effects of radical structural changes in the economy. This precluded the investigation of wider policy issues concerning, for example, the pressure exerted by multinational corporations for protection and preferential treatment within recipient countries and external effects such as the transfer of technology, the training of local personnel and the extent to which these companies encourage the growth of local ancillary industries.

Two major assumptions were made. Firstly that the most likely degree of local replacement of the foreign investment would be low, mainly because of the scarcity of indigenous entrepreneurs. In the absence of the foreign enterprise it was assumed that the demand would remain at the same level and therefore the shortfall in domestic supply would have to be met by imports. Secondly, it was assumed that in most instances the indigenous firm would use much the same techniques of production and have the same ratio of import costs to sales as the foreign firm.

Not surprisingly under these assumptions it was found that almost all the firms in the sample, 20 in Jamaica and 9 in Kenya, were found to have a substantial and beneficial effect on the balance of payments and national income of the host country. However the assumptions are probably realistic for a small economy in the early stages of development. As the authors point out, there are two forces acting in opposite directions in a small economy. Whilst a larger degree of potential local replacement would reduce the import saving of the foreign enterprise, the local firm would probably have to import most of the capital equipment and other inputs, and therefore the domestic value added would be quite low. This was reflected in the fact that the average effect on the balance of payments was fairly insensitive to large changes in the assumed degree of local replacement. One would not expect this to be the case for a larger and more advanced economy. In this case the possibility of domestic replacement would be greater, and a larger proportion of the direct and indirect demands generated could be met from domestic production rather than from imports. In addition a larger economy may have available, or be more aware of, the possibilities of some limited choice of techniques of production which would reduce the import coefficient, possibility at the acceptable cost of producing a slightly inferior quality article for the domestic market and for export to other developing countries.

The study also clearly illustrated the importance of examining combinations of characteristics rather than individual characteristics in isolation. For example if the foreign enterprise exported a large proportion of the output then the balance of payment effect would be strongly beneficial *provided* the direct and indirect import demands were low.

The discussion has so far centred on foreign direct investment in developing countries; however an additional and in recent years increasingly important source of foreign capital has been short-term loans, principally as *export credits*. These usually take the form of a firm exporting goods to a developing country and giving five years' credit, but with various risks including default, covered by the government of the exporting country. The importance of this source of finance can be judged from the fact that in the 1960s export credits increased fourfold, while other components of private flows increased by only 60 per cent. The basic disadvantage of the use of credits is that it means the use of short-term finance for long-term projects, and therefore quickly creates a serious debt service problem. Competition among suppliers has admittedly tended to lengthen the period of these credits, so that the majority today are for rather more than five years. In addition, nominal rates of interest are quite low. But as the Pearson report points out, low interest rates are often offset by high prices for the goods supplied. Thus unless these goods have a high social rate of return, the use of this source of finance will worsen the balance of payments position of the country.

4.4 Official aid
It may at first seem surprising that not all economists are agreed that official aid is beneficial to developing countries. Bauer for example regards it as a 'soft option' both for donors and recipients. For the former, because by giving aid they feel they can maintain high tariff barriers to protect their inefficient industries from competition from the LDCs. For recipients, because in the absence of aid they would be forced to achieve a better allocation of their resources and raise the rate of domestic savings. Friedman attacks aid because it strengthens the position of governments in LDCs which he believes are always subject to strong pressures to build prestige symbols of the modern industrial state. In addition, by giving these sums of money to governments their position is strengthened vis-a-vis the private sector, and the growth

of planning is encouraged to the detriment of the growth of a free market economy. At the other end of the political spectrum, official aid is seen as a powerful weapon of neo-colonialism.

In this brief appraisal it will be necessary to simplify what are complex arguments. Certainly the motives of donors are mixed and never explicitly formulated, ranging through the spectrum of economic, strategic and humanitarian reasons. As with all development issues in this book, the analysis of aid flows will be in economic terms, though as always this must not be taken to imply that this is the only, or even the most important aspect. A starting point is Mason's statement that it is a 'demonstrated fact that in at least a large part of the less developed world foreign aid can make, and has made, an effective contribution to economic development.' Flows of aid in the 1960s will be examined, some major defects in the quality of official aid will be indicated and possible future flows of aid in the second development decade will be considered. Finally, an examination is made of the use of quantitative models in determining aid requirements.

The politics of 'aid' have led to the term being applied in a way wholly different from its normal meaning. To illustrate this point, statistics for 1970 financial flows will be used, although it must be noted that the precise composition of these flows and their distribution between donors varies from year to year. Indeed it is a major cause of concern of the developing countries that official aid, which possibly finances as much as 40 per cent of imports vital to a long term development effort, may at any time be reduced because of short term balance of payments difficulties of a major donor. However with this qualification, the statistics indicate the order of magnitude of the policy issues concerning aid to developing countries.

Table 17
Flows of aid in $ US m

	net official and private		net official development assistance	
	1964	1970	1964	1970
UK	919	1,216	493	447
US	5,274	5,393	3,592	3,050
France	1,361	1,806	828	951
Germany	706	1,409	459	599
Japan	290	1,821	116	458
total of 16 DAC countries	9,645	14,701	5,957	6,808

Source Development Assistance Committee of OECD annual 'Review.'

Note These flows exclude grants by private charities

As may be seen from table 17, about 54 per cent of 'aid' flows in 1970 were actually composed of private investment in developing countries. Indeed in the period 1960-70 private capital flows to LDCs increased by 140 per cent whilst official development assistance rose by only 46 per cent. Even this increase in official aid overestimates its real growth, since the statistics are measured at current prices. When inflation in export prices and wages of technical personnel of the developed countries is allowed for, the real value of official aid only increased by 17 per cent over the past decade.

Table 18
Flows as proportion of GNP 1970

	net official and private[1]		net official development assistance	
	percentage of GNP	rank order	percentage of GNP	rank order
UK	1·0	6	0·37	8
US	0·55	16	0·31	12
France	1·24	2	0·65	1
Germany	0·76	8	0·32	11
Japan	0·93	6	0·23	13
Total 16 DAC countries	0·74		0·34	

Source DAC 'Review' 1971

[1] excluding grants by voluntary agencies

In terms of either total financial flows, official and private, or official flows alone, neither the US or the UK can be said to be carrying an unfair burden of aid as a proportion of GNP. These proportions must also be contrasted with the commitment by the development countries to give at least one per cent of their GNP, measured at market prices, in the form of aid by 1975. The Pearson Report calculated that if this target were reached by 1975 flows would increase to $23 billion at 1968 prices. The Commission also recommended that 0·7 per cent of GNP should be in the form of official development assistance. Again this can be contrasted with the 1970 average of 0·34 per cent.

These overall targets for aid flows certainly have the virtue of simplicity and would clearly lead to a substantial increase in volume, although one might argue that on the grounds of equity the targets should be progressive with income. More importantly, they do not deal with such central issues as the distribution of aid and inefficiencies in aid flows, which substantially reduce their real value.

Table 19
Major recipients of official development assistance

	official development assistance (average 1967/9) $ million	per capita ODA $	per capita GNP 1968 $
India	1,116·2	2·1	100
S Vietnam	509·6	29·3	130
Pakistan	456·8	3·7	100
Indonesia	422	3·7	100
Brazil	381·3	4·3	250
S Korea	321·9	10·6	180

Source DAC 'Review' 1971

In the period 1967-9, India, Pakistan, Indonesia and Brazil together received 35 per cent of official aid and yet have nearly the lowest levels of income and account for more than 50 per cent of the total populations of the developing countries to which the DAC countries give aid. To put the point another way, these countries averaged between 2 to 4 dollars of official aid per head of population, while comparatively richer countries such as Guyana, Guadeloupe, Martinique and Reunion averaged three hundred to six hundred dollars per head.

This imbalance arises from the overwhelming importance of *bilateral aid* in official flows.

Table 20
Flows of official aid by type 1970

	UK	US	France	Germany	Japan	total for DAC countries
official development assistance $m	447	3,050	951	599	458	6,808
percentage of ODA bilateral	89	87	89	78	81	83·5
percentage of ODA multilateral	11	13	11	22	19	16·5

Table 20 (cont'd.)

	UK	US	France	Germany	Japan	total for DAC countries
grants as percentage of ODA	50	50	73	54	39	57
grants as percentage of bilateral	50	52	80	53	32	58·6
grants as percentage of multilateral	54	40	56	62	10	49

Source DAC 'Review' 1971 figures calculated from, Table 6 of the 'Reveiw'

As may be seen from table 20, over 80 per cent of all official development assistance is bilateral and indeed, for the major donors, the proportion is nearer 90 per cent. It would be easy to conclude from this that much more aid should be multilateral, enabling it to be placed where it was most needed or where it would stimulate a higher growth of output, rather than the existing arrangement which determines that the bulk of aid flows to countries with which the donor has a special relationship. However, it can equally be argued that governments are keenly aware of the resistance of many people in developed countries to giving aid to developing countries. By granting it to a specific country and for that matter for a conspicuous project they are able to 'sell' the idea of giving more aid, and thus raise the flows to a level which would not be possible if the aid was multilateral and therefore anonymous.

A similar argument can be applied to *tying* aid either to a project and/or to purchases of goods and services from the donor country. This reduces the foreign exchange cost and thus allows countries in balance-of-payments deficit to give more aid. Aid tying can take a number of forms (see Bhagwati) and will have different economic effects on the recipient, but in general terms it will decrease the real value of aid if the donor country is not the cheapest world source of supply of the goods so tied. The value of aid is further reduced if the recipient has to buy from a monopolist, possibly created by the tying, or from a cartel specially formed to handle aid orders, since the price of the product will be further increased. In addition the donor may insist, as does the US, that the goods purchased have to travel in their ships at rates which are appreciably above world rates. Having acquired capital goods from the aid donor, the LDC will also have to purchase maintenance imports from this country for the whole life of the machine. Where the goods purchased are not capital goods or ones embodying a high degree of technology, tying purchases to the developed country may well inhibit the production and export of goods from another LDC.

It is difficult to estimate quantitatively these effects, but Ul Haq has demonstrated that in the case of Pakistan the effect has been quite substantial. From the reverse point of view, the UK Ministry of Overseas Development estimated the effect of small changes in the UK aid programme on the balance of payments for 1964-6; 'small changes' because otherwise the calculations would become cumbersome and have to include estimates of repercussions, such as LDCs defaulting on debt repayments, and retaliation by other aid donors. The study by Hopkin and associates is a good illustration of some of the problems in making a calculation of the balance-of-payments cost of aid. For example, the recipient of tied aid *may* have bought the goods from the donor even in the absence of the aid, and this probably applied to 62 per cent of the UK's fully-tied capital aid. On the other hand this 'switching' will probably be partly compensated by the recipient using the foreign exchange saved by the grant of aid to purchase additional goods from the UK. In addition, it was estimated that, for each £100 of UK aid, £21·5 was spent within the recipient country, thus raising income levels and hence imports, some of which would come from the UK. Also it was estimated that £38·1 out of every £100 of aid was spent on third country products, 'reflection' effects, thus raising incomes in these countries and hence imports to these countries from the UK in the normal multiplier manner. The estimate of these effects of a marginal £100 of UK bilateral aid is shown in table 21.

Table 21
Return to the UK of £100 of official aid

	£	£
apparent return in terms of tying		72·5
less switching	−18·9	53·6
plus induced imports	+ 4·1	57·7
plus reflection effects	+ 4·9	
	total =	62·6

Source Hopkin B and associates – 'Aid and the Balance of Payments' *Economic Journal* March 1970

To this must be added the return from multilateral aid, which increases by a certain multiple of UK contributions, and the geographical distribution which favours Britain. This is largely because India and Pakistan inevitably receive the greatest absolute amounts of this aid, and these countries traditionally trade with Britain. Thus for example for every £1 contributed by Britain to the International Development

Association (IDA) Britain enjoyed purchases of £1·5 in the period 1964-6. The overall short-term effect was to raise the 'aid-return' figure from £62·6 to £67. However it is possible that in conditions of limited capacity in UK industries the increased aid exports will be partly at the expense of exports that would otherwise have occurred. Deducting this capacity constraint, the aid-return to the UK became £58 for every £100 of official aid.

These figures, although subject to a wide margin of error, are certainly interesting in illustrating the balance-of-payments 'cost' to Britain of its official aid programme. The major contribution of the study however is in illustrating the complex economic reasoning behind such estimates. Even so, this still underestimates the future return to the UK from past, present and future aid, since it takes no account of debt service on loans to LDCs.

Table 20 shows the proportion of official development assistance which was actually given as a straight *grant* by major donors in 1970. France had the highest proportion with 73 per cent and Japan had the lowest with 39 per cent. Britain and the US gave just over half their official aid as grants. However, the rate of interest payable varied from 3·7 per cent for France and Japan to 1·2 per cent for the UK, with an average for the DAC countries of 2·8 per cent on all official loans. Now in calculating the actual aid given, allowance must be made for the fact that the rate of return on capital employed in the donor country will probably exceed the interest charged on the loan. This difference represents the *grant element of a loan.* To complicate the picture still further, it must also be realised that a grace period varying from 2 to 10 years, where no repayments are made, is normally granted. In addition to bilateral loans, multilateral agencies such as the World Bank, giving relatively 'hard' terms, and IDA, giving relatively 'soft' terms also lend to developing countries.

Debt in itself is simply a measure of one source of external finance which can be used to accelerate the growth of the economy, part of the proceeds of which would be used to service the loan. However, in view of the growth of bilateral and multilateral loans and particularly the rapid expansion of private export credits, it is hardly surprising that one of the major and increasing problems facing a number of developing countries is that of *debt service,* in some cases leading to a chronic shortage of foreign exchange and a disruption of the development effort. The public debt of the developing countries, which stood at $37 billion in 1966, had increased to about $66 billion by 1971, with a flow of debt service of $6 billion in 1970. It is of course ultimately the responsibility of recipients to limit the volume and structure of their debts to a realistic assessment of their capacity to service them. However, this must be appreciated in the context of the slow growth of official development assistance, the hardening of the terms of this assistance and the slow growth of a number of countries, export earnings,

Table 22
Some aspects of the debt service problem

	(1) per capita GNP 1968 $	(2) per capita GDP growth rate 1967-9 average	(3) growth of exports 1967-9 average	(4) adjusted 1-15 year average debt service as % of — exports 1967-9 average	(5) adjusted 1-15 year average debt service as % of — gross national savings 1967-9 average	(6) ODA 1967-9 — as percentage of imports 1967-9 average	(7) commerical borrowing average 1967-9 — as percentage of imports	(8) grant element of ODA 1967-9 average
India	100	3·1	5·4	19·2	6·6	40	7	79
Indonesia	100	1·1	10·1	26·3	29·8	39	3	63
Pakistan	100	4·2	6·9	29·4	16·7	37	14	67
Malawi	50	0·8	2·3	12·0	1,262·9	30	3	80
Greece	740	5·5	8·1	5·3	4·9	2	12	39
Iran	310	7·7	15·6	9·4	14·6	4	26	37
Malaysia	330	3·5	9·3	0·4	1·0	6	3	64

Source OECD Development Review 1971

Note columns (4) and (5) Debt service due in the first 15 years on outstanding debt adjusted for reserves in excess of 2 months imports.

column (8) Shows the face value of loans less the present value of scheduled debt service repayments discounted at 10 per cent plus grants, as proportion of official development assistance.

It is then hardly surprising that a developing country, trying to raise the level of per capita incomes in the face of a rapidly growing population, increasingly resorts to short term private export credits to finance long term development projects.

Table 22 shows some simple indicators of income and indebtedness and, to present some idea of the relative order of magnitude of the indicators, contrasts the debt service position of India, Pakistan, Indonesia and Malawi with that of Greece, Iran and Malaysia. Column 4, the debt service ratio, is the most widely used measure of the problem faced by a country and indicates the proportion of export earnings absorbed by debt service. The disadvantage of this indicator is that it presents a static picture of the immediate past and gives no indication of whether the situation is improving or not. In addition it presents only the external and not the internal factors of the situation, whereas a loan will always directly or indirectly provide some foreign exchange for its repayment. The question is whether this is in sufficient quantities and at the right time.

Ohlin demonstrates how quickly a reverse flow of funds can set in, even with moderate terms, and how long it can take to repay even small sums borrowed at low interest rates. Mikesell (ch 4) similarly demonstrates this 'snowball' effect. For example, with a gross lending of $100 per annum at (old) World Bank terms of 5½ per cent interest with 13 years maturity and a 3 year grace period, the $100 annual loan is reduced to zero after 9 years and to a net reverse flow of $47 per annum after 13 years.

As a result one method of assessing how much 'aid' should be given to a country is to determine its debt service capacity in terms of the gap between savings and investment over a period of years. Increased borrowing will of course raise the debt, but the increase in investment will raise income levels and, if the marginal propensity to save is sufficiently greater than the average, savings may eventually rise at a sufficient rate to close the savings-investment gap and hence enable repayment of the loan. However, the build-up of debt in the early years when investment was greater than savings must be included, and this clearly depends on the rate of interest and other loan terms. This approach has been summarised by Hayes in the critical rate of interest, i, where

$$i = r \cdot \frac{S_0 - S_1}{S_0 - kr}$$

where

r is the target growth of GDP (say 6 per cent)
S_0 is the average savings rate (say 12 per cent)
S_1 is the marginal savings rate (say 15 per cent)
k is the increment capital – output ratio (say 4:1)

On these values given in this example, the maximum rate of interest on loans that this unfortunate country could pay without the burden of debts becoming worse would be 1·5 per cent.

An alternative approach to assessing how much aid should be given is by constructing a *quantitative model* which will project over time the aid requirements of a country aiming to achieve self-sustained growth. A particularly sophisticated example of such a model is that by Chenery and Strout in which the need for foreign resources is determined either by the savings-investment or by the export-import gap, whichever is the greater. Of course, *ex post* the two must be identical, but *ex-ante* one may be larger than the other.

It must be appreciated that traditional analysis recognises only the savings-investment gap, so that if there is a balance of payments problem then this simply reflects too high a rate of absorption of goods and services in relation to the country's total output and net inflows of capital. The remedy must be to reduce the rate of absorption of the economy by increasing savings and decreasing investment until the excess demand is eliminated. Provided the correct exchange rate and fiscal and monetary policies are adopted the balance of payments problem will be resolved, for the decrease in aggregate demand, in addition to lowering the demand for imports, will also release resources which, given the 'switching' effect of the devaluation of the exchange rate, will directly and indirectly increase the supply of exports and import substitutes.[1] Thus if a country is faced with balance of payments difficulties then this simply reflects a mis-allocation of resources and it is not a valid reason for giving additional foreign aid.

The objections to this analysis are twofold. In the first place the process of adjustment will inevitably take some considerable time in a developing country given the state of markets, thus foreign capital will be required to enable the growth of output to be maintained and to accelerate the re-allocation of resources. In addition a developing country may well be unable at the margin to transform sufficient domestic resources released from additional savings into increased exports, because of rigidities and imperfections in world markets; or into import-substitutes, because it would be too costly given the small size of the market or because they are unable to achieve the advanced technology embodied in the product. This concept of a *structural* balance of payment problem will be examined in chapter 5. For the present it is sufficient to appreciate the strategic role which foreign assistance may play in providing resources which could not be produced in the developing country and the foreign exchange

1. This is a very greatly simplified account of a complex and still unresolved problem of analysis. For a good summary see Clement, Pfister and Rothwell, Chs. 5 and 7.

which could not be earned by increased exports. The provision of this foreign assistance enables a greater utilisation of domestic resources and thus a higher growth rate than would otherwise be the case.

Chenery and Strout see most, though not necessarily all, countries passing through three phases in the process towards self-sustained growth. Initially, they predict a skill limitation on growth, shown by an 'absorptive-capacity' limit to the level of investment which is below the level required to sustain the target rate of growth. In this phase, aid will assist the country in increasing the amount of investment at a rate greater than the target rate of growth of output, until the required level is reached. At this point, or some time before it, the second phase will appear, with an increasing gap between the domestic rate of investment and the (lower) rate of savings. Again, since the aim is self-sufficiency then, for the amount of capital inflow to decline, the marginal savings rate must be greater than the required investment rate. Now during this period it is assumed that the associated trade gap can be filled by the LDC, but certainly towards the end of this period this will become increasingly difficult, for the reasons previously mentioned. Thus for ultimate self-sufficiency, the marginal import ratio must be less than the average, through import substitution, and/or the rate of growth of exports must be greater than the target rate of growth of output.

This model gives aid donors a number of criteria for judging performance as aid recipients move towards self-sustained growth, depending on which phase they are judged to be operating in. In addition, Chenery and Strout apply the model to a large number of LDCs and find that the successful countries, according to their criteria, have had a growth of exports greater than the target growth of output, and conversely that there was no example of a country which had, by means of import substitution, for long sustained a growth of output greater than its growth of exports. An additional criterion is therefore suggested, that performance during trade-constrained growth should be judged by export performance.

The model has been subject to considerable criticism.[1] In particular, it is said that savings in LDCs are so erratic and the statistics so imperfect that it is pointless to make the marginal savings rate a key variable. To meet this problem, Maizels has adapted the model to an *ex post* one in which savings is the residual. The model however does allow the investigation of the different outcomes resulting from different amounts and forms of aid, the effects of varying policies and standards of performance by recipient countries, the likely effects of varying external conditions, and so on. A particularly interesting result emerges in applying the model to Pakistan: by giving the economy the maximum amount of aid it could absorb in the early years, Pakistan

1 For a good summary, see Mikesell.

could achieve self-sustained growth quicker. Thus, over the whole process, Pakistan required less aid than if it had been given in smaller quantities over a longer period of time.

Perhaps one of the most thoughtful criticisms of such models has been put forward by Eckaus who shows that the concept of self-sustained growth is deceptively simple since it involves certain implicit value judgements and the need to make inter-country comparisons.

This brief survey has shown various imperfections in the quality of aid and in particular trends to minimise the significance of the often repeated phrase about the 'burden to aid' supported by developed countries. Clearly improvements are required not only in the total flow of real development assistance, but also in its composition.

One interesting proposal covering both quantity and quality is that of the *link*.[1] In its 'organic' form this consists of allocating a proportion of the annual issue of special drawing rights (SDRs) to an international agency such as the World Bank who would then use them to finance development projects in LDCs after exchanging them with central banks for useful currencies. Clearly the importance of this scheme to developing countries would depend on the amount of SDRs allocated, but if SDRs were to eventually replace individual currencies as a reserve asset, then the benefits would be substantial in the sense that it would be a larger volume of untied multilateral aid at concessional terms which would broadly increase automatically with the increase in world production.

A strong reason for being optimistic about the eventual acceptance of the scheme is that it would also assist the developed countries in overcoming a fundamental dilemma of the present international economy. Pressure is being exerted on the US to substantially reduce its balance of payments deficit. For its part the US is anxious to reduce the level of unemployment, partly by raising the rate of growth of its exports. If this were to occur then the current balance of payments surplus of other developed countries would of course be reduced. However these countries have sound reasons for believing that the marginal productivity of resources is higher if devoted to exports than if allocated to meeting internal demand (for instance because at the margin, demand will probably be predominantly in the lower productivity service sectors). Thus even if full employment is maintained by substituting domestic demand for the loss of exports, it will also entail a slower growth of real incomes, which in turn will create a different set of social and economic problems. In other words the developed countries wish the US to reduce its balance of payments deficit yet at the same

1 I am grateful to Professor G. Maynard of the University of Reading for the ideas expressed in this section.

time they are unwilling to accept the corollary that for this to occur other countries' trade balances must deteriorate and their growth rates probably be reduced.

This dilemma could be avoided if the link proposal were adopted, for it would allow the LDCs to finance an increased balance of payments deficit and thus by contributing to an expansion of aggregate world demand it would help to accommodate the substantial rise in US production and exports (of the order of 25 per cent of the 1971 level of exports), which is required. The benefits of the *link* to the developed countries would go beyond the transitional period in which the US improves its balance of payments, for in the long run it could provide an effective substitute for the US deficit, which, as has been argued above, has underpinned the levels of employment and growth of the past decade.

In the long run, undoubtedly the main advantage to the developing countries of a major improvement in the international monetary system is that it would remove a fundamental reason for the developed countries, raising and maintaining barriers to international trade.

references and further reading

P T Bauer and B Ward   *Two views on aid* London: Institute of Economic Affairs Occasional Paper No 9 1966

J Bhagwati   *The tying of aid* UNCTAD Secretariat TD/7/Supp 4 1967

R J Chelliah   *Fiscal policy in underdeveloped countries* London: Allen and Unwin (2nd ed) 1969

H B Chenery and A M Strout   'Foreign assistance and economic development' *American Economic Review* 1966

M Clement, R Pfister and K Rothwell   *Theoretical issues in international economics* Boston Mass.: Houghton Mifflen 1967

J H Dunning and R D Pearce   *UK investment in developing countries* London: Political and Economic Planning (forthcoming)

R S Eckaus   'Economic criteria for foreign aid for economic development' in J Bhagwati and R S Eckaus (eds) *Foreign aid* London: Penguin Modern Economics Readings 1970

M Friedman   'Foreign economic aid: means and objectives' *Yale Review* 1958

Mahbub Ul Haq   'Tied credits − a quantitative analysis' in J H Adler (ed) *Capital movements and economic development* International Economic Association New York: Macmillan 1967

J P Hayes   'Long run growth and debt servicing problems' in Avromovic *'Economic growth and the external debt'* Baltimore, Johns Hopkins Press 1964

B Higgins   *Economic development* (2nd ed) London: Constable 1968

B Hopkin and associates   'Aid and the balance of payments' *Economic Journal* 1970

G C Hufbauer and F M Adler   *Overseas manufacturing investment and the balance of payments* Washington: US Treasury Department 1968

N Kaldor   'Role of taxation in economic development' in EAG Robinson (ed) *Problems in economic development* London: Macmillan 1965

I M D Little   'Tax policy and the third plan' in Rosenstein-Rodan (ed) *Pricing and fiscal policies* London: Allen and Unwin 1964

A Maddison   *Economic progress and policy in developing countries* London Allen and Unwin: 1970

A Maizels   *Exports and economic growth of developing countries*
                 Cambridge UP 1968

E S Mason   *Foreign aid and foreign policy* New York: Harper and Row
                 1964

G Maynard   *'Economic development and the price level'* London:
                 Macmillan 1962

G M Meier   *The international economics of development* New York
                 and London: Harper and Row 1968

R Mikesell   *The economics of foreign aid* London: Weidenfeld and
                 Nicolson 1968

L Needleman   *Balance of payments effects of private foreign investment*
                 UNCTAD TD/B/C/3/79 Geneva 1970

G Ohlin   *Aid and indebtedness* Paris: OECD 1966

L Pearson   *Partners in development,* London: Pall Mall 1969

A R Prest   *Public finance in underdeveloped countries* London:
                 Weidenfeld and Nicolson 1963

V K R V Rao   'Investment, income and the multiplier in an under-
                 developed economy' *Indian Economic Review* 1952

B Reddaway   *UK private overseas investment in developing countries*
                 Cambridge UP 1967

chapter 5

exports, import substitution and economic integration

5.1 The complementarity between the three policies

The application of the Chenery-Strout dual gap model to the LDCs indicated that the successful countries had experienced a rate of growth of export earnings greater than the growth of domestic output, and conversely that countries emphasising policies of import substitution had not succeeded in removing the foreign exchange constraint on growth. This result conforms with the belief of many economists, at least in the developed world, that LDCs can only accelerate their rate of growth through increasing exports. As a general statement this certainly seems reasonable, considering that of the hundred or so developing countries just under three quarters have populations of less than 15 million and an average of 5 million. Of the remainder, India dominates with over 500 million, and then comes a substantial gap until Brazil, Indonesia, Nigeria, Pakistan and Turkey with between 60 to 130 million. The majority of LDCs therefore have small populations, low levels of income per head concentrated in the hands of a few people, and a very small exchange sector. It follows that the size of the domestic market will be so small as to make impossible the establishment of the minimum, far less the optimal, size of plant in most manufacturing industries without the creation of considerable excess capacity and consequently high unit costs.

Industrialisation policies must therefore aim to provide both for the domestic and the export market, and in this sense the debate between import substitution and export diversification is a meaningless one for most developing countries. The problem is that the industries cannot become established and competitive at one and the same time, and therefore there is the classic case for protection of the import industry during the 'learning' period when the skills of management and labour are being improved and when economies of scale are beginning to appear. But, as has been noted, the domestic market is usually so small that for most industries even the smallest plant would operate at high cost. To overcome this obstacle the LDCs have moved towards an integration of their markets, at the same time protecting themselves against competition from the developed countries. In addition, they have pressed the developed countries into lowering their tariff barriers for a limited 'learning' period on goods in which the developing countries have a potential comparative advantage. It is important therefore to regard export promotion, import substitution and integration, as to a large extent complementary rather than alternative policies, all aimed at raising the rate of growth of output and employment.

It is possible to argue of course that LDCs have many other objectives than simply maximising the growth of output and employment over time. Johnson (1965) and Cooper and Massell for instance have specifically constructed models in which the country obtains satisfaction from having some industry, independently of the satisfaction they derive from the consumption of industrial products. Protection could certainly be justified in these terms, but policy makers must be aware of the cost in terms of output and, in the long run, employment foregone.

5.2 Exports as an engine of growth
Ultimately then there is a strong case for as 'open' a development process as possible, since the economy will increasingly require imports of goods from the developed countries to sustain the expansion of both the agricultural and industrial sectors, as well as satisfying part of a probably increased propensity to import from rising incomes. Maizels, in a study of the export performance of 10 sterling area developing countries for the period 1951-61, found that the long-term elasticity of investment with respect to a unit change in the capacity to import ranged from 0·7 to 1·0 in 6 of the 10 countries studied (the remaining 4 countries' results were not significant). This relationship worked first through the increased availability of capital goods, and this in turn influenced the level of domestic investments. Aid and private foreign capital will certainly assist, but for most countries this source of foreign exchange will provide only a small proportion of requirements, and, as emphasised in chapter 4, much of this foreign capital has to be repaid with interest in hard currency. A relatively open economy will also assist in the productive allocation of resources, since domestic producers will have to compete with imports, while exporters will not have the protection which transport costs give to the home market.

For all these reasons it is therefore a matter of concern that, in the period 1950-67, the LDCs achieved an annual growth of export earnings of 4 per cent, less than half that of the developed countries. The share of LDCs in world trade therefore declined from 27 per cent in 1953 to 19 per cent in 1967.

5.3 The export experience of the developing countries
The reasons for this disappointing performance of exports in the face of a rapid growth of world trade are to be found in the economic policies pursued by the developed and less developed countries, and the composition of the exports of the developing countries. As the Pearson Report stated

'Almost ninety per cent of the export earnings of the developing countries derive from primary products. Moreover, nearly half of these countries earn more than 50 per cent of their export receipts from a single primary product. As many as three-quarters of them earn more than 60 per cent from three primary products.'

The value of exports of primary products, excluding petroleum, grew by only about 2 per cent per annum in the period 1953-67. In addition these exports were subject to considerable *instability*. For instance, Maddison found that for this period the average fall in export receipts of LDCs from peak to trough was 28 per cent; for developed countries the average was only 7 per cent.

Of course, not all primary producers are developing countries nor for that matter have all LDCs who are primary producers experienced a slow rate of growth combined with instability of their export earnings. So far as growth of export earnings is concerned, an important consideration is whether a country produces a large proportion of the world trade in a commodity, for in this case the world price and income elasticity of demand for the product will approximate to the price and income elasticity of demand facing this country. A good example is the case of Brazilian coffee. Conversely, if a country contributes only a small proportion of the world trade in a commodity, for example Kenyan coffee, then it can take the elasticity of demand as being close to infinity at the world price.

Despite these important qualifications, a causual relationship can be shown between the preponderance of primary products in the exports of LDCs and the slow rate of growth and instability in the export earnings of these countries. As mentioned in chapter 3, if the primary product is a foodstuff both price and income elasticity of demand will be low in accordance with Engels Law. If it is an industrial raw material, price elasticity of demand will be low if it constitutes a small proportion of total costs, and income elasticity of demand will also be low due to the effect of technical progress in the developed countries. The latter has consistently taken the form either of reducing the proportion of inputs of raw materials relative to a given quantity of output, or of creating synthetic substitutes for the raw material.

Maizels found that the consumption of synthetics has increased at double the rate of the consumption of natural raw materials, affecting particularly rubber and fibres, with very severe effects on the export earnings of developing countries in the sterling area in the period 1951-61. He estimated that the continued encroachment of synthetics would reduce the net imports of natural materials into the industrialised countries by 10 to 20 per cent by 1975, depending on the assumption adopted for the growth of output in these markets. In addition to these demand factors, the price elasticity of supply may also be low due to long gestation periods in production. This will certainly be true of plantation crops, which take 3 to 5 years to mature, and for extractive industries. In addition, once large sums of capital have been sunk in these enterprises, producers will continue to sell on the market so long as the low variable costs are being covered and some contribution is being made towards fixed costs. Under these conditions variations in demand will not be reflected in supply, and so there will be large fluctuations in prices and earnings.

This analysis has provided the basis for the thesis of Raul Prebisch, formerly head of the Economic Commission for Latin America (ECLA) and later Secretary General of the United Nations Conference on Trade and Development (UNCTAD), that the LDCs have suffered from a deterioration in their terms of trade over various periods within 1879-1953 and 1950-61. The deterioration, for primary products relative to manufactures, was of the order of 26 per cent, and for LDCs relative to developed countries it was 17 per cent. Prebisch extended the foregoing analysis of slow growth and instability by asserting that primary product prices fell further, relative to manufactures, in the downswing of the cycle than they rose in the upswing. This took place because, for institutional reasons, manufactured goods' prices are 'sticky' in a downward direction, particularly because of the greater prevalence of monopoly power in the developed countries. This greater monopoly power also extends to the labour market where powerful trade unions take gains in productivity in the form of higher money wages. Primary producers on the other hand have taken gains in productivity in the form of lower prices particularly because production was, and to a large extent still is, controlled by foreign enterprises seeking to obtain low-cost inputs, and also seeking to avoid controls over repatriation of profits by giving artificially low values to the exported commodity. This thesis was particularly important during the first UNCTAD meeting in 1964, as it provided the basis for the argument that the developed countries should compensate the LDCs for the loss incurred by this long-term trend.

The argument certainly appears persuasive, but unfortunately suffers from some very important defects both of a conceptual and statistical nature. There is a good summary of the theoretical difficulties in an article by June Flanders. Conceptually, we cannot draw any conclusions about trade gains and losses from movements in the prices of imports and exports, that is from the commodity terms of trade. Export prices may fall while import prices remain constant but it is still possible to be better off, provided there has been a more than proportional increase in the quantity exported. The capacity to import is shown by the income terms of trade, commodity terms of trade multiplied by the quantity of exports, although even these are not strictly a measure of the gains from trade. Statistical criticisms abound, but probably the most important are that in measuring the terms of trade in the late nineteenth and early twentieth century Prebisch, due to lack of statistics for LDCs, took the reciprocal of the UK terms of trade as being those for LDCs. Apart from UK imports being a mixed bag of products, and not all primary products, from various countries, not all of them LDCs, UK import prices fell because of a dramatic fall in transport costs. Secondly, movements of the terms of trade are highly sensitive to the terminal years chosen and, by starting one of his sub-periods in 1950, Prebisch started his trend in a year of abnormally high primary product prices, due to the Korean war, and ended in a year of depressed prices due to a recession in the US.

For present purposes the capacity to import, the income terms of trade, is the most significant measure. Wilson, Sintra and Castree studied movements in the *commodity* (N) and *income* (I) terms of trade for the period 1950-5 to 1962-5. They found that N had increased by 10 per cent for developed countries, and fallen by 9 per cent for the LDCs. However, significantly from the point of view of the foregoing conceptual criticism of Prebisch, they found that I had increased for both groups, although by considerably more for the developed countries which recorded a rise of 136 per cent, than for the LDCs, which increased by 57 per cent. Within the broad group of LDCs there were large variations. Thus, for Peru, I more than doubled while N fell by 20 per cent. Brazil showed no improvement in N, while I fluctuated considerably.

Part of the explanation of the slow growth of export earnings of developed countries relative to the expansion in world trade is thus in terms of the commodity concentration of their exports. Diversification of exports by product and market is therefore an obvious solution. This has been prevented in part by the policies pursued by the LDCs themselves but at least as much also by the policies of the developed countries.

After the complete collapse of international trade in the 1930s, the developed countries sought to regulate the international monetary and trading system to prevent a repetition of such a disastrous series of competitive tariff barriers, devaluation, and general 'beggar-my-neighbour' policies. Thus the International Monetary Fund (IMF) and the General Agreement on Tariffs and Trade (GATT) were formed soon after the second world war. The basic principles underlying GATT are those of *reciprocity*, equal reductions in quotas, tariffs etc, between member countries, and *non-discrimination*, giving all other countries the same terms as given by a country to its most favoured nation, the 'MFN' principle. These rules implicitly assume that bargaining will be among equals, but in practice it will be dominated by countries with a large and heavily protected market and therefore something worthwhile to offer the other party, and also with a good competitive position in world markets and therefore something to gain by negotiating. It is therefore hardly surprising that the interests of LDCs have been largely ignored in post-war tariff reductions. In fact most of the trade concessions negotiated have been on fairly sophisticated capital-intensive goods of interest only to the developed countries. Admittedly tariffs on some non-competing primary products have been appreciably reduced, but, given the maintenance of tariff structure which escalates with the degree of processing of the raw material such tariff reductions actually worsen the future export prospects of the LDCs.

To appreciate this point, consider the difference between the *nominal tariff*, the percentage tax levied on the price of the imported product, and the *effective tariff*, which measures the tariff as a percentage of the value added by that stage of production. For example, assume the following

raw material costs £5 per ton and carries tariff of 10 per cent,
processed form of raw material costs £10 per ton and carries tariff of 10 per cent,
raw material accounts for 50 per cent of the cost of production.

Then the nominal and effective tariffs are identical at 10 per cent. However, if the tariff on the raw material is reduced to zero, then the whole weight of the £1 tariff on the processed form is falling on the £5 value added by processing. Thus the percentage by which the costs of production at this stage of fabrication in the domestic, protected, industry can exceed those of the foreign competitor is raised to 20 per cent. (The calculation is actually more complex than this, but the principle remains the same.) In other words the effect of reducing the tariff on the raw material to zero was to double the effective tariff barrier which the LDC has to overcome to export the processed product to the developed country. *Ceteris paribus,* the smaller the cost of processing the higher will be the effective tariff, increasing by a large multiple of the escalation in the nominal rate. This concept is especially important when considering the barriers facing LDCs trying to accelerate their development in the most obvious manner, namely by processing the exported raw material.

Balassa estimated the effective tariff on a number of commodities, and an example was copper ore which carried a tariff of 0·10 per cent in the UK, zero in the EEC. On copper wire the nominal rate in the UK was 10 per cent and in the EEC it was 3 per cent, but the effective tariff on wire was 77 and 23 per cent respectively. Textile fabrics in the UK carried an effective tariff of 42 per cent; primary steel an incredible 99 per cent; and consumer goods on average a 24 per cent nominal rate and 40 per cent effective rate. To estimate the effect of the removal of these tariff barriers is very difficult because there are so many other restrictions on trade, and we do not know the price elasticity of supply in the relevant LDCs, but it would appear that given their lower labour costs, and in some cases abundant sources of raw materials, they could benefit considerably. Balassa estimated that exports of manufactures by LDCs to the UK, EEC and Japan could increase by 30 to 40 per cent, and to the US by more than 50 per cent.

In addition to tariff discrimination against the LDCs, there has developed a whole range of *non-tariff barriers*. The complete battery of tariffs, quotas, subsidies and commodity 'agreements', all sanctioned by the special clause of 'market disruption' to the principle of non-discrimination, have been used by the developed countries to protect their high-cost agricultural producers against competition from the LDCs. Cotton textiles are a similar example of such comprehensive restrictions on exports from the LDCs. The development of EFTA and the EEC provide additional examples of discrimination against LDCs in the sense that they favour trade with member countries through the *trade diversion* effect. Developed countries also discriminate in favour of certain LDCs and therefore against others through the operation of preference schemes such as Commonwealth Preference, and the 'illegal' preferences granted by the EEC to certain LDCs. While such special arrangements certainly exclude non-member LDCs, the extent to which they actually harm their export earnings of primary products is not clear, since for a number of commodities such as coffee and sugar there is excess capacity, and therefore open competition could well lead to price collapse.

The conclusion that GATT has been the 'rich man's club' therefore seems reasonable. Dissatisfaction with the operation of international trade reached a head in the early 1960s, culminating in the United Nations' Conference on Trade and Development (UNCTAD) in 1964, which was virtually given over to discussing the report by Prebisch, *Towards a new trade policy for development.* (For a full discussion see H G Johnson, 1967a). After analysing the problems facing LDCs in increasing their exports, Prebisch put forward six major proposals; compensatory finance for deteriorating terms of trade, commodity trade agreements principally aimed at raising world prices, tariff preferences on certain products for a limited period of time on the basis of so-called *infant industry* arguments, regional integration among LDCs, increased trade between LDCs and the centrally planned economies, and lastly the establishment of UNCTAD as a permanent UN institution.

A *compensatory financial scheme* was started by the IMF in 1963 which allowed members to make additional drawings, if necessary over and above the normal limit of 200 per cent of their quota, of up to 50 per cent of their quota, if they experienced a shortfall in their export earnings. This scheme, while useful to LDCs, is essentially geared to short-run balance-of-payments crises. Prebisch wanted a long-run commitment which was really a disguised form of aid, but by tying this to commodities Prebisch made it an unacceptable burden to countries like the UK which import a significant proportion of commodities from LDCs. Eventually the UK and Sweden proposed a *supplementary finance fund* whereby the developed countries would contribute to a central fund, administered probably by the World Bank, which would be used to guarantee, after scrutiny, the foreign-exchange component of their planned investment.

This proposal is clearly of greater use to LDCs than the short-term measures of the IMF. It would also appear to be superior to individual commodity agreements which, in their unhappy history, have been shown to be difficult to administer due to the essential conflict of interest between producers and consumers, especially in determining the long-run price level, and to the cost and difficulty of holding stocks, especially of perishables. However, this proposal was still under study by the World Bank in 1972. Commodity agreements could, by providing compensation, perform the essential task of inducing surplus producers in both developed countries and LDCs to transfer their resources into other directions, but this probably assumes too high a degree of co-operation among countries.

Proposals for a Generalised System of Preferences (GSP) were finally produced in June 1971 when the contracting parties agreed to waive the provisions of article 1 of GATT for a period of 10 years, for products originating in the developing countries. To date the 17 OECD countries and New Zealand have produced detailed schemes of preferences. These are very complex because each developed country or group of countries in the case of the EEC have individually drawn up lists of tariff preferences and exclusions. In addition they have stipulated safeguards which seek to protect domestic producers from strong competition from imports from developing countries and also to protect developing countries who already have special arrangements with the preference giving country. In general terms, the scheme applies to manufactures and semi-manufactures with exceptions mainly in the field of textile, petroleum and petroleum products, leather and leather goods. While the prime purpose of the scheme is to accelerate the growth of developing countries by promoting industrialisation and raising the level of their exports of manufactured goods, the developed countries have also given preferences to selected primary products. Thus the list of preferences for the major trading countries appears as follows:

UK	69 items of which 21 are primary commodities
US	95 items of which 45 are primary commodities
EEC	50 items of which 12 are primary commodities
Japan	59 items of which 19 are primary commodities

The depth of the tariff cut varies considerably. For example the UK grants a zero duty on all products listed, with the exception of about half a dozen which will receive the Commonwealth Preference rate. The EEC grants a zero duty on all industrial products listed with small cuts in the full tariff rate on listed processed agricultural products. Japan is even less generous for 57 of its 59 products will only have the duty reduced by half.

The picture is completed by outlining the safeguards written into the agreements to prevent 'excessive' imports from the developing countries. Some countries such as the UK have been content to introduce escape clauses, the restrictiveness of which remains to be seen. However other countries, notably Japan and the EEC, have imposed *a priori* limitations. For example the EEC have a complex system of ceilings and quotas. The ceilings are expressed for each category of products and are set at a level equal to the value of the Community's imports of the product from beneficiaries in 1968 (excluding those already benefiting under Associate status), with a supplement which is set annually and at present is fixed at 5 per cent of the value of imports from non-beneficiary (developed) countries. No beneficiary can provide more than half the ceiling. In addition quotas have been set for 'sensitive' products such as textiles and the maximum amount of the quota from any one country ranges from 10 to 50 per cent. Finally, both the UK and the EEC reserve the right to amend their schemes if developing countries with which they have special trade relationships are adversely affected by the GSP.

It is of course too early to attempt a detailed analysis of the benefits of the scheme to developing countries. However certain aspects are of immediate concern. On the one hand, the theory of effective protection indicates that the cuts in nominal tariffs could bring substantial benefits in expanding the export earnings and promoting the industrialisation of the developing countries, provided the latter adopt appropriate internal policies. On the other hand, as Johnson (1967(b)) points out, the magnitude of the tariff reduction is not a measure of the potential gain to developing countries. Developed countries have imposed high tariffs not only to protect comparatively high cost domestic producers, but also to protect their balance of payments. In this case a high tariff simply reflects a high price elasticity of demand for the imported product. This point must be linked to the fact that a number of products, where the LDCs have the most obvious potential comparative advantage, have been specifically excluded from the preference schemes. It must also be remembered that the GSP has only been agreed to for a period of 10 years. If the scheme were highly successful in substantially raising the exports of manufactured products of LDCs, then the developed countries might decide to re-impose the tariff to protect domestic producers and to protect their balance of payments. The possibility of such action after the 10 year period, and of the developed countries resorting to the escape clauses during the 10 years, must certainly inhibit the expansion of investment in manufacturing exports in developing countries.

An additional cause for concern relates to Britain's entry into the Common Market, since the less developed members of the Commonwealth will loose their preferential position in the UK market. It appears that some Commonwealth African countries will be able to apply for 'association' with the EEC, while the Caribbean Commonwealth countries will be able to negotiate trade agreements for particular products, including sugar. For the remaining LDCs, including the large numbers of people in the Asian Commonwealth countries, there seems little prospect of being granted more than the preferences under GSP. The question then arises whether Britain will adopt the EEC schemes with its restrictive ceilings and quotas and which exclude some important processed primary products, which the UK includes in its preferences.

Clearly the Generalised System of Preferences will benefit the developing countries and, to the extent that they replace higher cost sources of supply, the scheme will also benefit consumers in the developed countries. However the potential benefits must be heavily qualified by the restrictive character of many of the schemes, while if they only operate for 10 years and tariffs are re-imposed then a new set of problems will have been created.

While the protectionist policies of the developed countries have been of major importance in limiting the growth of exports of the LDCs, the domestic policies of LDCs have also been important in determining their success or failure in increasing their exports. Table 23 gives some indication of this factor.

Table 23
Annual growth of export earnings in selected LDCs

	1950-3 to 1960-3 per cent	1959-60 to 1966-7 per cent
Brazil	0·17	1·3
India	0·1	2·7
UAR	− 0·1	1·9
Greece	23·0	12·0
Taiwan	11·0	20·8
Nigeria	5·0	6·7
Argentina	0·16	5·5
Turkey	0·6	6·0
Pakistan	1·0	8·3

Source IMF International Financial Statistics

Brazil, India and the UAR have consistently recorded slow rates of growth in export earnings while Greece and Taiwan (not including 'special' cases like Hong Kong and Israel) have consistently recorded high rates of growth of exports. Argentina, Turkey and Pakistan have shown considerable improvement in recent years over the previous period.

A more detailed analysis has been conducted by De Vries of 29 LDCs for the period 1950-3 to 1960-3, which showed that for a number of countries the deviation in actual export earnings for 1960-3 was as much as 60 per cent from that predicted on the basis of constant 1950-3 market shares. As theory would predict, countries with small market shares fared better than those with large shares. De Vries also tested the significance of domestic variables such as financial management, reflected in price inflation, and resource allocation, as reflected in agricultural and industrial growth rates, and found that export performance in both agricultural and manufactured commodities was positively correlated with the growth of agricultural output, while export performance was relatively poor in countries with strong inflation. The conclusion seems to be that countries with a slow growth rate of exports should diversify their export base either by entering into primary product markets in which their output will be a small proportion of the total, or, like Israel, Mexico, Spain, Yugoslavia and Taiwan, into manufactures where their output will inevitably be a small proportion of the total.

It is often argued that this policy cannot be practised by large countries because the developed countries will immediately raise trade barriers. Perhaps this view is too pessimistic, for one could hardly call Pakistan, with a population in excess of 100 millions, a small country yet it has succeeded in raising the proportion of manufactures in total exports from one per cent in 1953 to almost 50 per cent in 1966. Too pessimistic a view of world markets, combined with the temptations of a large internal market, possibly explain the disappointing export and growth performance of countries like India and Argentina. For countries like Ceylon, Thailand, Colombia and Malaysia, with small domestic markets and quite large shares in particular commodity markets, this problem appears much more serious since 'policy' is to a far greater extent exogenously determined.

5.4 Import substitution

Motives for import-substitution policies vary considerably, but the belief that the defects of international trade, outlined above, have resulted in a shortage of foreign exchange which has curtailed the growth of the economy has certainly been the dominant influence. Fundamentally, the encouragement of import-substitution industries is a *growth* strategy aimed at accelerating the growth of the economy above that determined by export receipts. Even in the absence of a foreign-exchange constraint, import substitution can be justified by the compelling need in most LDCs to provide employment for the large numbers of urban unemployed, the underemployed, and the inevitable increase in the labour force arising from past increases in the population, as well as to raise the growth of per capita income. As has been outlined in chapter 3, governments have often seriously underestimated the ability of the agricultural sector to increase both output and employment at low capital and foreign exchange cost, when given the correct incentives and additional resources. However, granted this, there still remains a strong case for the protection of import substitution industries, especially in a reasonably populous country with a level of per capita income which is relatively high by the standards of LDCs.

The need for protection is based not only on the classical infant industry argument, but on a wider recognition of the market imperfections and structural rigidities of LDCs which cause a sharp divergence between *social* and *private* costs. The classical case for protection rests on the existence of economies which are external to the firm but internal to the industry, such as the creation of a skilled labour force. Development economists such as Rosenstein - Rodan and Nurkse have developed this further by pointing out that a single manufacturer will not survive on his own because most of the income generated by the investment will be spent on the output of other sections of the economy such as food, clothing and housing. However, if a large number of industries which are complementary in a final consumption demand sense are established simultaneously, they will become each other's customers and 'supply will create its own demand'. This is therefore an argument for protection on a horizontal basis depending on the income elasticity of demand.

This *balanced growth* approach has been sharply criticised, because the size of the development effort needed to create simultaneously such complementary consumer-goods industries would be far in excess of the resources available in the developing country. To put the point another way, if the country could mount such a development effort it would not be underdeveloped in the first place.

In contrast, Hirschman sees the major constraint on development as being the shortage of entrepreneurs able to recognise, and take advantage of, profitable investment opportunities. To overcome this constraint the government must deliberately *unbalance* the economy by creating industries, such as steel, with strong backward and forward linkages, which will virtually compel additional investment decisions in the private sector. As experience in such decision-taking grows, so the government will be able to withdraw and leave the private sector to take the 'hard' as well as the 'easy', induced, investment decisions. This is, therefore, an argument for protection in depth rather than horizontally; it is also an argument favouring rather more investment in industry and rather less in agriculture, in that the former has stronger backward and forward linkages, and therefore will induce a higher level of investment. Presumably Hirschman would also be willing to run the 'hard' investment choices at a loss because the externalities are so great. While the analysis is very interesting, one cannot help thinking that as a policy it is rather like Russian roulette; if the policy does not succeed in inducing investment the result could be a collapse into hyperinflation.

A further argument put forward by Lewis to justify tariff protection of industry is derived from the existence of *surplus labour* whose marginal product is low (to Lewis it is zero), but due to institutional factors such as strong trade unions the wage rate is appreciably in excess of the marginal productivity of labour. To this extent the unskilled urban wage rate will exaggerate the loss of agricultural output from employing the additional worker in industry, with the result that the industrial sector will be smaller than that required for the optimal allocation of resources.

The problem with all these arguments for protection is that, owing to the difficulty of deriving even an approximate value for the externalities and to the divergence of costs from true resource costs, they can be used to justify almost any pattern of investment. This is not to say that they are necessarily unimportant, or that they should be ignored, but simply that these special factors should be treated with caution and allowed to qualify, but not supplant, normal economic calculations. This matter is further discussed in chapter 6. As Little and his associates emphasise in their recent study of import substitution in 6 LDCs, these are arguments for specific subsidies to industry, rather than for a general system of tariff protection, which also has a number of undesirable side effects such as inhibiting the growth of exports and causing too high a level of capital intensity with the result that the growth of employment is unnecessarily reduced. The study concentrates on the experience of Brazil, India, Mexico, Pakistan, the Philippines, Taiwan and Argentina. These countries were selected because of their history of import substitution, in some cases dating from the collapse of the international economy in 1929, and the consequent desire of these countries to become less dependent on international trade. The result was that after 15 to 20 years the process of import substitution became increasingly difficult and now constitutes a barrier to economic progress. There has been a proliferation of firms with considerable excess capacity, and therefore high costs, behind high tariff barriers. The average rate of effective tariff protection exceeds 200 per cent for India and Pakistan, 100 per cent for Argentina and Brazil, 50 per cent for the Philippines, and 33 and 25 per cent for Taiwan and Mexico respectively. Indeed, in some cases protection was so high that the value of input at world prices was in excess of the value of output at world prices, although both the level of protection and the value added varied considerably both between industries and over a relatively short period of time.

These countries have also used overvalued exchange rates or multiple exchange rates, which act as general taxes and subsidies. In the former case it is a tax on exports and a subsidy to imports while the latter method, although being more sophisticated in its distribution of taxes and subsidies, requires continuous administration especially in an inflationary situation. Overvaluation of the exchange rate also requires the rationing of foreign exchange to avoid balance-of-payments deficits which cannot be financed from reserves or additional aid.

Decisions on what goods to import and where to invest require a wealth of information which the planning authorities have not the time or the personnel to gather, thus they come to rely on 'rules of thumb'. Industrialists in turn have come to calculate what will be the next changes in government policy, rather than what the market requires. Delays inevitably occur in the administration of these controls and thus firms react by hoarding scarce materials and indenting for more than they require, since the alternative is the underutilisation of capacity due to the shortage of foreign exchange. Overvaluation of the exchange rate, often combined with unrealistically low rates of interest, has also resulted in a pattern of investment which is too capital intensive, with the result that the growth of employment has often been less than that required to absorb the rapid increase in the urban unemployed.

High industrial costs, and therefore high prices, by turning the internal terms of trade against agriculture, have accelerated the drift of population from the villages to the towns. In addition, the converse of cheap capital for industry is high interest rates in rural areas which, combined with relatively low prices, have often retarded rural investment with the result that labour productivity is kept low in agriculture, thus further contributing to the disparity in the growth of incomes. Of course the imbalance would eventually be self-correcting with the consequent rise in food prices, but governments have intervened to prevent this inflation by compulsory purchases etc. There is of course no inevitable link between industrialisation and these growth retarding features. They result from over-investment in the wrong kind of industries. That industrialisation is a necessary part of development for most LDCs is beyond dispute and, as the experience of Taiwan and Pakistan in recent years has shown, the right kind of industrialisation can also expand export earnings and in addition, as a result of diversification, place these earnings on a much more stable basis. What Little and associates clearly demonstrate is that generalised protection will inevitably result in increasing government intervention with a series of stop-gap measures. The conclusion is that the inefficiencies of market prices in allocating resources are best dealt with by means of specific measures, such as the direct subsidisation of the wage bill, compensation for externalities and so on.

An interesting and detailed study has been made by Baranson of the vehicle industry in developing countries, which amply illustrates the general points made above. For example, the aim of the Argentine government was to save foreign exchange by domestic manufacture of vehicles. The latter objective was achieved during the period 1959-65 but at the cost of a five-fold increase in foreign exchange costs, as well as doubling the price of vehicles compared to the freely imported product. The causes of this disastrous result were not hard to find, with 'thirteen manufacturers producing over 68 cars and trucks'. In addition, there were 'several thousand component and parts manufacturers in Argentina, many operating out of small garage shops as sub-contractors to larger parts of manufacturers' p. 46). This resulted in high costs and also lack of standardisation and poor quality. Baranson describes this proliferation of models as a sort of 'hog cycle' reaction to a small market.

The experience of countries which have pursued import substitution policies for some years calls into question their use as a strategy for accelerating development. Certainly, for the first 20 years or so, these policies probably accelerated the growth of the Latin American economies and certainly led to a fall in the ratio of imports to national income. In recent years, however, the average propensity to import has remained constant or has even increased, while growth has slowed, in some cases, as in Argentina, to the point of stagnation. As Felix explains, part of the reason is undoubtedly that in its initial stages such industrialisation is relatively easy, substituting for imported consumer goods whose efficient production is on a relatively small scale, and which does not demand a high degree of skill and technical knowledge. Industries like steel in which there are considerable economies of scale, are also viable because they derive their demand from a wide variety of sources. However, as import substitution continues into more sophisticated capital and intermediate goods whose demand is derived from quite specific sectors of the economy, the constraint of the size of the market and supply of skills begins to appear. In addition, an increasing amount of inputs will have to be imported to sustain the industry and thus the domestic value-added will be small, as well as being vulnerable to shortage of foreign exchange. It is possible that eventually the capital output ratios will rise to such an extent as to negate the original foreign exchange savings. Also, as Felix points out, it is probable that as incomes rise consumers will demand an increasing proportion of imported goods, especially more sophisticated and better quality goods, a shift in demand which may well be accelerated by the international 'demonstration' effect of the high standard of consumption in the rich countries. Under these conditions there is a return to the situation where growth is determined by the level of export earnings and net foreign capital flows. To avoid this situation import substitution policies must take a more sophisticated view of the structure of production than simply selecting those items which figure prominently on the import bill. The interdependence of production throughout the economy and of the pattern of investment, with the resulting composition of consumption, must be appreciated. Fundamentally, import substitution must act in such a way as to shift the composition of final demand towards a lower import intensity.

5.5 Economic integration

As emphasised earlier, the majority of LDCs have small populations as well as low levels of per capita incomes. Thus the constraint of the size of market will quickly appear in industrialisation policies. An obvious solution is, therefore, to go beyond the artificial bounds of the nation state and form a larger market, either as a free trade area, a customs union or a common market. By trading amongst themselves, LDCs can also save 'hard' currency for the import of capital and intermediate goods from the developed countries.

Integration will have two main effects. On the one hand, the elimination of tariffs will *create* trade between members, based on comparative advantage, and thus raise incomes. On the other hand, reducing tariffs between members results in discrimination against non-members, and thus *diverts* trade from a possibly lower cost source of supply to a higher cost (member) source. On this basis maximum advantage will be gained from integration if foreign trade is a small proportion of national income, hence the possibilities of trade creation will be large, and correspondingly small for trade diversion. In addition, what foreign trade there is should, before integration, be between members, hence minimising trade diversion. The economies concerned should also be similar in structure, thus furthering competition and ensuring that only the least-cost firms survive.

On all these criteria for successful integration the LDCs come out badly. Trade is typically a large proportion of national income and mostly with developed, non-member, countries. However, this does not mean that there will necessarily be substantial trade diversion, for many of the goods imported from and exported to developed countries could not be purchased from, or sold to, other LDCs.

The fundamental weakness of customs union theory is that it is static, though this is not to say that it is irrelevant, and concerned with the optimal allocation of resources given the existing structure of the economies. Essentially, the LDCs are interested in changing the existing structure by using the integration of markets to establish viable industries which do not at present exist. In addition, to the extent that these industries utilise resources, such as labour, which would otherwise remain idle, then there is a clear gain. It must also be appreciated that, rightly or wrongly, LDCs will insist on certain industries being established and, to the extent that economies of scale are present, this will be at lower cost in an integrated framework than in each separate country.

Evidence on the extent to which economies of scale exist in manufacturing industries is conflicting, but they appear to be quite general in the initial costs of most plants, particularly in capital intensive industries, and they appear to be significant even in operating costs. Chenery in his study of 42 countries in 1953 and 53 countries in 1958 found that, between countries having the same level of per capita income, value added by manufacturing increases by about one-eighth more than in proportion to the size of population, reflecting the effects of market size and economies of scale. It should also be remembered that the larger the market the smaller the growth rate needed to provide a profitable investment opportunity. Expectations of investors may, therefore, improve and thus increase the total volume of investment.

A major problem arises over the allocation of investment between members, especially if not all countries are equally attractive to investors. An example of such problems is provided by the enormous differences in size of populations and levels of per capita incomes between members of the Latin American Free Trade Area (LAFTA). At the extreme the least attractive member may have to divert imports from low cost sources of supply to high cost partner countries but gain no additional investment in return. Budget transfers as compensation are unsatisfactory, except to mitigate short-run discrepancies in gains from integration. In this respect, therefore, it is probably better if the economies are initially complementary. Alternatively, a free trade area could be formed thus enabling the minimum trade diversion, since the 'unattractive' country could allow the free import of goods it did not wish to manufacture itself and thus minimise the preference given to its partner countries.

Effective integration will also probably depend on the development of new communication links between members as existing communications will probably have been developed between sources of supply and markets, particularly export markets in developed countries, and not between neighbouring developing countries.

As yet the experience of integration among developing countries is limited notably to the East African Common Market and LAFTA, but its potential benefits would appear to be considerable among a number of groups of countries, both in lowering the cost of industrialisation and in providing a competitive base for diversifying exports, and in this way accelerating the growth of output and employment.

references and further reading

B Balassa	'Tariff protection in industrial countries: an evaluation' *Journal of Political Economy* December 1965
J Baranson	*Automotive industries in developing countries* World Bank Staff Occasional Paper No 8 1969
H B Chenery	'Patterns of industrial growth' *American Economic Review* 1960
C A Cooper and B Massell	'Towards a general theory of customs unions for developing countries' *Journal of Political Economy* 1965
B A De Vries	*The export experience of developing countries* World Bank Occasional Paper No 3 1967
D Felix	'The dilemma of import substitution - Argentina' in G F Papanek (ed) *Development policy theory and practice* Cambridge Mass: Harvard UP 1968
J M Flanders	'Prebisch on protectionism: an evaluation' *Economic Journal* June 1964
A Hirschman	*Strategy of economic development* New Haven: Yale UP 1958
H G Johnson	'An economic theory of protectionism' *Journal of Political Economy* 1965
H G Johnson	*Economic policies towards less developed countries* London: Allen and Unwin 1967(a)
H G Johnson	'Trade preferences for developing countries' *Lloyds Bank Review* April 1967(b)
W A Lewis	'Economic development with unlimited supplies of labour' *Manchester School* 1954
I M D Little, T Scitovsky and M Scott	*Industry and trade in some developing countries* London: Oxford University Press 1970
A Maddison	*Economic progress and policy in developing countries* London: Allen and Unwin 1970
A Maizels	*Exports and economic growth of developing countries* Cambridge UP 1968
R Nurkse	*Problems of capital formation in underdeveloped countries* Oxford: Blackwell and Mott 1953

P Rosenstein Rodan   'Industrialisation of eastern and south eastern Europe' *Economic Journal* 1943

T Wilson, R P Sinha and   'The income terms of trade of developed and developing
J R Castree   countries' *Economic Journal* December 1969

chapter 6

development planning[1]

6.1 Introduction
In many cases, considerable state intervention in the workings of the market is advocated to solve the problems of LDCs. For this intervention to be effective, the government must have some overall plan to ensure reasonable consistency among policy instruments such as taxation, interest rates, trade controls etc; among policy objectives such as the growth of output and employment; and between policy instruments and policy objectives. Before discussing development planning it would perhaps be useful to recapitulate some of the important reasons why planning and government intervention are considered to be an integral part of the process of accelerating development.

6.2 The case for planning
The strength of the case for government economic planning, and the type of planning required, will clearly vary as between developing countries, but broadly speaking the argument in favour of planning will consist of the following elements.

(a) Imperfections in factor and goods markets result in prices failing to reflect real resource costs.

(b) Of more fundamental importance, even perfect competition will not allocate resources efficiently in the context of development because of the importance of externalities.

(c) A shortage of Schumpeter's 'dynamic, risk-taking entrepreneurs' who have the knowledge and ability to seek out potentially profitable investment opportunities means that the government must create obviously profitable opportunities which virtually 'force' the investment decision.

(d) Alternatively, the social cost of 'bribing' the reluctant investors may be considered too high, in which case the government must directly undertake the bulk of the investment programme.

1 See JN Robinson *Planning and forecasting techniques: an introduction to macro-economic applications* London Weidenfeld and Nicolson 1972 for a full account of planning methods.

(e) A plan may be essential for attracting foreign capital.

This last reason for planning is sometimes referred to in a derogatory fashion by anti-planners. This attitude is puzzling since a well-thought out plan, which shows the part which foreign aid and private investment will play in the overall development of the economy seems eminently sensible. However, criticisms of planning in developing countries will be examined later. For the moment the case for planning is examined in more detail, with particular reference to the importance of externalities.

A significant feature of many of the obstacles to the acceleration of development has been the existence of externalities which cause a gap between the private and social product. For example in chapter 2, when discussing the economic effects of a rapid growth of population, it was noted that at least in the initial stages of development it is quite rational for parents to desire a large family even though rapid population growth was clearly detrimental to the development of the economy as a whole.

One of the most important effects of externalities concerns individual investment decisions. For instance, in most LDCs the decision to build even a moderate sized steelworks will represent an appreciable addition to the capital stock of the country. The significance of this is that when assessing the potential profitability of the enterprise, it is not possible to make the usual and necessary *ceteris paribus* assumption of partial analysis. If the additional output of steel results in a lower market price, which is likely in a protected market, then there will be immediate external benefits to those using steel as an input, thereby enabling them to expand their output by charging a lower price for their product. Owners of factor inputs used by the steel industry will also benefit from the increased demand for the services. Thus, as Scitovsky shows, such an investment decision will lead to producers' and consumers' surpluses which the initial investor cannot capture through the price charged for his output. A further consideration is that the investment, by increasing the size of market, will create further investment and employment opportunities. External economies are particularly large in the case of investments in social overhead capital. As pointed out in chapter 3, the provision of adequate transport and communications, by linking more closely consumers and producers, can benefit the economy enormously by enabling sufficient price incentives to be given to agricultural producers without causing urban price inflation. However, given the underdeveloped state of the economy, the large minimum size of the investment and the fact that the size of the returns will be highly uncertain, depending as they do on other people's investment decisions, and recouped over a long period, there is a very real danger of under-investment in areas which will be potentially productive in the long term, and over-investment in areas which offer an obvious immediate return. Similarly, private under-investment will almost certainly occur in the provision of health facilities and education. A particularly important example of this is the creation of a skilled labour force, where the benefits from providing such services cannot be recouped by the supplier through the price he charges, because the value of such services is not readily quantifiable, and because the consumers are probably too poor to pay a price which would reflect the true value of the service provided. To summarise, a case for state intervention can be based on the fact that in most LDCs the stock of skilled labour and social overhead capital is small, and consequently an addition to these resources will not be marginal. As a result, the initial set of prices will not measure the true social profitability of investment in these assets. The government however is in a central position to take into account the essential interdependence of investment decisions and consequently to estimate the social, as distinct from private, costs and benefits.

In addition to the appreciable external economies which derive from many investment decisions in the majority of (small) developing countries, a case for government inter-vention also rests on the prevalence of a situation in which money costs are significantly in excess of real resource costs. As was argued in chapter 1 in the case of dualism and in chapter 5 in justifying protection, wages paid to unskilled labour will exceed the opportunity cost of this labour. Wages will be determined by the need to attract both the worker and his family on a permanent basis from the agricultural sector to the industrial sector, and will therefore be equal to the average product of agricultural labour plus an incentive premium to induce migration. In addition wages will probably be further raised by trade union pressure and possibly by political pressure for minimum wage regulations. If however there is 'surplus' agricultural labour then the social opp-ortunity costs of providing additional industrial employment, although positive (because the marginal product of re-allocated agricultural labour will be small but positive, and in addition there will be the social cost of maintaining the worker and his family in an urban environment), will be appreciably smaller than the industrial wage paid.

Money cost will also diverge from real resource costs in the provision of capital to the rural sector. Even allowing for the possibility of high risks in investing capital in the agricultural as opposed to the industrial sector, and for the high administrative costs of a large number of small loans, rates of interest are often unjustifiably high. This is usually the result on one hand of the all-pervading need for credit by cultivators and on the other of the localised monopoly power of credit suppliers. The position of the latter is often strengthened by the government attempting to accelerate industrial development by making capital cheap and plentiful in the industrial sector. The widespread over-valuation of exchange rates in LDCs is another example of imperfections in the price system, this time encouraging relatively capital-intensive industries (because imported capital goods are unrealistically cheap) producing for the domestic market (because the profitability of exporting has been unrealistically depressed).

It has been shown that market forces will not efficiently allocate resources towards investment, particularly in LDCs, and since institutional factors cause further distortions in market forces the conclusion is that comprehensive development planning is required to accelerate economic development. The case for a comprehensive as opposed to a piecemeal policy was further discussed in chapter 4 in examining the central part which the government must play in raising the marginal savings rate. This will mostly take the form of increasing taxation to reduce the growth of consumption but, as was stressed in chapter 4, a purely revenue approach, by ignoring the effect of taxation on the allocation of resources, may well reduce the ability of the economy to grow. Thus from the point of view of the finance of development, a comprehensive approach seems desirable. As was also mentioned in chapter 4, a good development plan which clearly indicates investment opportunities to the private sector will encourage private investment by both the indigenous population and from overseas. Both bilateral and multilateral aid donors usually insist on a fairly comprehensive plan which will show both the projected foreign-exchange requirements of the country concerned, and the place of the projects which are being financed, in the overall development of the economy. Finally, as discussed in chapter 5, the slow progress made towards economic integration and the small benefits which appear to have resulted from existing schemes have largely been due to a failure to draw up a comprehensive investment programme which will avoid the wasteful duplication of productive capacity and share the benefits from integration on some agreed basis among member countries.

6.3 Conflicts in development policies
It has been implicit in much of the analysis that the objective of economic development is to maximise the growth of output. Clearly countries may seek a number of other objectives, such as the reduction of unemployment and under-employment, a more equitable distribution of income, both between individuals and over the various regions of the country, and a greater degree of economic independence through a reduced reliance on international trade and foreign capital flows. In addition, the development strategy chosen will crucially depend on the time element. If a country wishes to be independent of substantial foreign capital flows in, say, 10 years time, then to have any hope of success it must severely restrict the growth of consumption over this period and ert almost the whole of the increase in resources to capital formation. In this way the country will, by the end of the 10 year period, have sufficient productive capacity to finance the desired rate of growth without depending on foreign capital. If economic

independence is sought by the end of 25 years, the requirements for curtailing the growth of consumption will be less severe. If, on the other hand, the objective is to maximise the growth of output over the next five years, then the pattern of resource allocation will be very different. Emphasis will be placed on quick-yielding forms of investment even though they may also have a short life. Stated more formally the latter policy implies using a high discount rate on all new investment projects, thus favouring industries using techniques of production with a high ratio of current output to capital employed, light industry, and where there is a choice of techniques within an industry choosing those techniques which use the minimum amount of capital for a given output, for example favouring roads as opposed to railways.

Some development objectives will be more or less complementary to each other, but others may well be in direct conflict. For example, the objective of a rapid growth of employment opportunities, by shifting the distribution of income towards wage earners, will also probably be consistent with a policy of a more equal distribution of income. However if the marginal propensity to save of wage earners is assumed to be substantially smaller than that of profit earners, who also invest all their savings, such a policy will directly conflict with that of maximising the growth of future output or of economic independence. Conflicts may also arise between policy instruments and policy objectives. For example, the government may wish to increase the marginal propensity to save by increasing taxation but this may conflict with the objective of a more equal distribution of income since, in practice, due to institutional constraints such as a weak administration and political opposition, the bulk of the increased revenues may have to come from goods of mass consumption, as discussed more fully in chapter 4.

A development plan must also be *feasible* in the sense that resources can be reasonably expected to be available when required. Thus a given set of policy objectives and policy instruments used to attain these objectives, will result in a particular pattern of demand for natural resources, financial resources, capital goods, skilled manpower and imports. The supply of these resources constitutes the principal structural limitation on the attainment of the economic goals of society.

6.4 The planning horizon

At the risk of labouring the point the essential interdependence of policy decisions has been stressed, and also the fact that once policies have been implemented they often have long-term effects which are difficult to reverse. A long-term perspective plan is therefore required to clarify the basic objectives and development strategy. As well as providing the framework for more detailed plans, the perspective plan will provide the basis for investment in social overhead capital which typically has a long gestation period, that is, a long interval of time between the initial investment and subsequent output. One particularly important example of this is the need to make decisions both on the amount and the composition of investment in education, considerably in advance of the needs of the economy for skilled labour. The length of this gestation period, typically 20 to 25 years, will thus partly determine the time-horizon of the long-term perspective plan. Within this broad framework more detailed medium-term plans will be drawn up, usually for a 5 year period, outlining a consistent set of policy objectives, the means by which these objectives will be attained and the implications of this for the various sectors of the economy. Finally the one year short-term plan will set out in detail the specific sectoral requirements and, if necessary, provide the authority for the government to carry out its specific functions in the plan.

6.5 The use of policy models in development planning

Policy models are essentially a greatly simplified, aggregated representation of the operation of the economy under the influence of a number of policy instruments which seek to direct the economy in such a way as to achieve the economic goals of society. The model is constructed by listing the economic goals of society, drawing up a set of equations which will describe the present structure of the economy and defining the policy instruments which are available to control the direction of change of the economy. Finally, realistic values are attached to those, exogenous, variables which will influence the economy but which can be considered as being pre-determined by external forces. In practice an *ad hoc* procedure will be followed in constructing the model.

The goals of a society will vary but policy makers will have some general idea of what the economy could achieve in the way of the growth of output, consumption, employment, decreased dependence on foreign capital flows etc. The first stage is simply to list these objectives. After the model has been worked through, it can be seen to what extent they have to be modified. The purpose of a policy model is not to specify a particular combination of output, employment and so on, but to describe a feasible area, given the structure of the economy, exogenous variables and constraints, within which the decision-maker can select a particular set of values or goals. In other words a policy model shows the opportunity cost of attaining one objective in terms of the under-attainment of other objectives.

Since this is an aggregate model there will only be a relatively small number of equations describing the technical and behavioural conditions of the economy. For instance the aggregate production function may simply make output dependent on the size of the capital stock, on the assumption that capital is the limiting factor of production and therefore other factors of production will always be in sufficient supply.

This relationship would then be shown by an incremental capital-output ratio (ICOR) which, as the name implies, simply shows how many additional units of capital are required to produce a unit increase in output. There are usually a set of equations describing supply and demand conditions in the labour market and another set showing the factors determining the level of savings and net capital formation. An import function will also have to be included and ideally an export function, although exports may be assumed to be exogenously determined. The structural equations are then complemented by the usual set of macroeconomic identities.

The policy instruments available cover the familiar range of fiscal and monetary variables such as taxation policy, which will partly determine the propensity to save, the exchange rate, the rate of interest, the size of foreign capital inflows, and the rate of discount, a high rate implying a preference for 'present' as opposed to 'future' consumption. The government may be free to select any range of values it wishes for some policy instruments, such as the exchange rate, but other instruments, such as tax rates, will only be free to move within a certain range for institutional and social reasons.

One of the immediate problems in constructing policy models is that there is usually a large number of factors which could potentially affect the growth of the economy. The problem is to identify the effective limitations, and the only practical method is by trial and error. Thus a potentially effective limitation on growth is incorporated into the model and run on the computer. If a particular constraint is seen to have a significant effect on a policy objective and is not the result of statistical errors or mis-specification such as assuming a function is linear when it is non-linear, then this limitation is built into the model.

One of the questions that should always be asked of policy models is how accurate are their predictions. One might claim that the more aggregated the model the more accurate the prediction, simply on the basis of errors cancelling one another. On the other hand, the usefulness of a model for policy-making increases the greater the degree of detail. How then is it possible to produce a model which forms a useful basis for policy-making and yet also produces reasonably accurate forecasts?

One method is to construct sub-models of those factors which are found to be important limitations on the growth of economy. For example, the growth of the export sector may be found to be a crucial determinant of the growth of the economy. In this case it would be appropriate to build a sub-model of the export sector in order to examine, for instance, the effect of different trading policies and different assumptions, with regard to future trends in world commodity markets, on total export receipts. The results of this model will then flow into the main aggregate model, showing the implications of these results for the economy as a whole. Modifications made in the main model as a result of this information will in turn flow back into the sub-model and so on. Sub-models will have weak links with each other and essentially can only be related to each other via the main model. The advantage of this method is that it avoids the wasteful construction of a large model which in the end may fail to produce useful results. The splitting-up of a model in this way also helps the model-builder to appreciate exactly why he obtains a particular result from certain assumptions.

A particularly important criticism of model-building in developing countries refers to the stability of the parameters such as the marginal propensities to consume, import and save, the incremental capital-output ratio, the growth of labour productivity and so on. ICORs are particularly unstable in developing countries, depending as they do on the ability to make use of excess capacity, the availability of inputs in short supply, particularly if imported, and the efficiency of management. In this respect the model constructed by Chenery and Bruno for the economy of Israel represented an important advance in recognising that a particularly important limitation on growth in a developing country will be the composition of demand. As was emphasised in chapters 3 and 5, every investment decision results in a change in the composition of final demand. In a developed economy with a diversified industrial structure such effects are not important for they can easily be absorbed through a marginal reallocation of resources. However, in a developing country with a much simpler industrial structure and a severe shortage of foreign exchange, such shifts in the composition of demand have to be studied to see whether they can be met either through domestic production or through imports. If the demand cannot be met then a different development programme is required. The composition of demand should not only be looked at in this negative sense, because a higher growth of output with given supplies of capital may be achieved by shifting the composition of demand towards industries with considerable excess capacity. In terms of the model, this action would then result in a fall in the observed ICOR. Similarly, since labour productivity will vary between industries, a shift in the composition of demand towards industries with a high level of labour productivity will raise this parameter of the model. To take account of these important changes, Chenery and Bruno incorporated a sub-model of inter-industry flows within their main aggregate model of the economy.

Having satisfactorily constructed the policy model, the next stage is to use the model to illustrate the development alternatives facing the country. Values are therefore given to the instrument variables, the exchange rate, marginal savings rate, proportion unemployed, capital inflows, government expenditure, determined by what is considered realistic from a political, economic and administrative point of view. Given that these are informed guesses, the best method to deal with this uncertainty is to pick a range of values ranging from pessimistic to optimistic, as shown in the model of population growth in chapter 2, and for aid flows in chapter 5.

The model can then be solved for the various assumptions of the instrument variables and the results of altering these assumptions seen in terms of the effect on the policy objectives. The model will also be valuable to policy formulation in identifying the effective limitations on development.

As Chenery and Bruno emphasise, an aggregate model contains an optimistic bias in its presentation of development alternatives. Thus the model may imply that an industry will have to expand output by an apparently modest amount, but more detailed information on the industry may show that this modest target cannot be attained because of a shortage of a particular type of skilled labour. At a more general level a modest export target may be unrealistic because it implies a massive expansion of manufactured exports, given a stagnant market for primary commodities which constitute a large proportion of total exports. Chenery and Bruno employed an input-output table to determine the feasibility of the aggregate model and, as already mentioned, also used the results to determine alternative values for the parameters, such as the propensity to import under different values of the exchange rate.

Planners must go one stage further and study individual projects. As well as giving detailed information on the feasibility of the plan, such as the demand for particular skills, the assessment of the discounted costs and benefits of an individual project shows whether resources are being used economically. In view of the imperfections in factor and goods markets in developing countries, these costs and benefits must be valued at 'accounting prices' which broadly reflect the resource use and benefits of the project.[1] Interaction will then take place between the aggregate model and the project analysis. Some projects will need to be enlarged or contracted because aggregate demand is larger or smaller than initially assumed. Conversely the aggregate model may have to be altered because project analysis shows the plan is not feasible or makes a wasteful use of scarce resources. Project analysis may also indicate that the trade-off between employment creation and growth may not be as harsh as first thought, because possibilities exist for substituting labour for capital in the production functions. Lewis (1966) draws the useful distinction between innovation which has improved the quality or uniformity of the product or economised on raw materials, and improvements which have merely substituted for labour, such as mechanical transportation, packaging, and book-keeping. Plants could be redesigned in developing countries to include the former and exclude the latter.

1 Further details on estimation can be obtained from the OECD *Manual of Industrial Project Analysis,* vols I, II & II, Paris 1968.

In many respects the planning framework presented here is a highly idealised one which does not exist in such a comprehensive form in any developing country in the world. In India where comprehensive planning has developed over the past 20 years and planning on public investment aggregates and the incorrect belief that only 'investment', nothing like the degree of sophistication outlined is reached. Certainly their macro-economic plans are very sophisticated yet, as Streeten and Lipton emphasise, small scale planning at village and project level barely exists. This results in a concentration of planning on public investment aggregates and the incorrect belief that only 'investment', and not consumption, produces growth and that there is necessarily a conflict between a more equal distribution of income and growth. Concentration on physical investment has also resulted in a neglect of the human factors in economic development, which again can only be assessed at a local level.

Thus, while the theoretical case for planning in developing countries is very strong, and powerful techniques of analysis exist to assist plan formulation, the experience of planning is dismal. The extent of the failure of planning to accelerate economic growth can perhaps be indicated by referring to recent statements by two eminent economists, with wide experience in the field. Waterson states that 'by far the great majority of countries have failed to realise even modest income and output targets in their plans except for short periods. What is even more disturbing, the situation seems to be worsening instead of improving as countries continue to plan'. Lewis (1969) states 'the failure of planning is that there has been no correlation between development planning and economic growth. That is to say, the countries which have grown most rapidly have not been the countries which have had the most elaborate plans'.[1]

6.6 The reality of planning in developing countries
What are the reasons for this extraordinary gap between the theoretical potential of development planning and the reality of its failure? Assessments of the failure of development planning are strongly biased by the initial point of view. Those who believe that comprehensive planning, utilising the most advanced techniques devised by the econometrician, is a powerful weapon for accelerating development, attribute the failures of planning to technical failures associated with the formulation and implementation of the plans. A second group of economists however take a more sceptical view of the problem and regard comprehensive planning as worse than useless in the present state of developing countries, although such planning could be useful at some time in the future. A third group, while accepting the need for government planning, discount the

1 This absence of correlation of course does not prove that planning has been irrelevant, since many factors other than planning will operate on growth.

need for comprehensive planning at any stage of development. Instead they draw the conclusion that decision-taking is so complex that it is more efficiently carried out through the operation of market forces, despite their deficiencies in developing countries.

From a technical point of view one of the most important reasons why plans have not been implemented, lies in the common separation of plan formulation from implementation. This results in the common characteristic of plans providing detailed information on what is to be achieved but having very little to say on the means by which these objectives are to be attained. As emphasised in the outline of a policy model, making plans in isolation from means and a consideration of feasibility is almost certain to be a waste of time. This gap between formulation and implementation is partly the result of a lack of interest on the part of planners in descending from the esoteric heights of model building to the more mundane level of small-scale planning and project appraisal. A similar attitude also probably explains the emphasis on industrial development and the neglect of simple and high-yielding forms of investment which often exist in the agricultural sector, but which can only be discovered by those with a reasonable knowledge of the agricultural environment. Equally important has been the isolation of planners from the centres of policy making. Again, as pointed out in the description of the utopian model, information should flow freely from those formulating the plan to those making the policy decisions, so as to achieve the reconciliation between conflicting assumptions and expectations. All too often information flows only in the other direction.

A more wide-range attack on comprehensive development planning and model building is that, given the inaccuracy of the statistics used, the diversity of objectives including non-economic objectives and the restrictive assumptions underlying its techniques, comprehensive model building is pointless. Indeed given the heavy demands it makes on scarce and highly skilled manpower, the opportunity cost of this futile exercise is very high.[1] One reply is that policy decisions have to be made regardless of the quality of statistical information, and they are better based on a model which illustrates some of the major consequences of the decisions reached than by using some partial 'rules of thumb'. But the operation of the model may compound the statistical errors. The effects of errors in the statistics on the predictions of the model can be examined by using sensitivity analysis. This simply means giving a range of values to the exogenous elements and parameters of the model and observing the degree to which the results of the model are altered. If the model is sensitive in this sense the quality of the prediction is correspondingly reduced; but such an outcome is by no means necessary, and in any case the test will serve to indicate the most fruitful lines of improvement in

1   A good example of such criticisms appears in an article by Vernon.

statistical information. Such a defence of model building leaves, as Vernon points out, the fundamental problem that past experience and analogies with the experience of other countries offer little guide in selecting the relevant range of any variable. In addition, the sensitivity of the model will also probably depend on the combination of ranges tested together. This criticism would appear to be particularly valid with respect to the effect of technical change and import substitution upon the domestic coefficients. Model builders can certainly go a long way towards incorporating these effects into the model, but all too often highly simplistic and misleading devices are resorted to. Fór example, the incorporation of technical change into a model by assuming that the country imports the 'best practice' of the developed countries will perpetuate the incorrect assumption of zero substitutability between capital and labour and hence the belief that the economy has a sharp conflict between the growth of output and employment. For the reasons stated earlier, there would appear to be appreciable scope for the substitution of labour for capital even in such apparently capital-intensive industries as steel production. It should be clear however that this is an argument against particular model builders, and not against model building as such.

There is however, a long way to go in coping with the problems of risk and uncertainty, which are almost certainly greater in a developing than in a developed country. Basic statistics on the structure of the economy are inadequate, and the projection of key components such as agricultural output and export earnings will initially be subject to a wide margin of error.

Criticism of model building goes further than this, for Vernon questions the relevance of consistent, comprehensive and optimal models to the needs of developing countries. A development plan may well be drawn up solely to justify a claim for foreign aid, and discarded afterwards. The plan will almost certainly perform the vital political role of providing a rallying point of the support of the electorate. For this to be successful everyone must seem to gain, a criterion which may well conflict with the economists' insistence on consistency. These points are obviously valid, but it must be remembered that by ignoring consistency the politician will only gain support for a very limited period of time. Inevitably the performance of the economy will fall short of expectations, resulting is dissatisfaction with planning in general and the government in particular. The point still remains that the consistency of a model involves judgement on the future values of the parameters, and in this sense consistency is a matter of faith, not inevitability. Again this is an argument against excessive trust in the forecast and not against models *per se.*

With regard to optimality, it has been demonstrated that policy models need not, and indeed should not, claim to provide an optimal solution, since this immediately involves the problems of constructing a social welfare function. It is far more fruitful to use the model to determine a feasible decision area for the policy maker, within which the trade-offs between policy objectives can be indicated.

The third set of criticisms of detailed planning implemented by control methods claims that such methods will be especially difficult and inefficient to apply in a developing country. For a statement of the argument see H.G. Johnson. The attraction of the use of market forces is that it is automatic, requiring no large administrative machinery and central decision making which will be at the mercy of vested interests.[1] Certainly there are inefficiencies in market forces in developing countries, but these can be mostly dealt with by government policies which correct these inefficiencies without assuming the responsibility for allocating resources. It has certainly been argued throughout the book that the extreme assumptions of perfectly inelastic demand and supply curves with respect to price changes do not stand up to the evidence. The additional argument against the use of the price system is that it will lead to an undesirable distribution of income since growth will depend on the distribution of income being shifted towards profit earners. That is, even if it is accepted that the allocative efficiency of markets is superior to that of central direction, reliance on markets will conflict with the objectives of social justice. It is possible however that this conflict exists more in the minds of armchair theorists than in reality. Certainly the discussion of traditional farmers in chapter 3 resulted in the conclusion that there existed considerable scope for low-cost methods of raising the output of the majority of cultivators, provided reasonable price incentives were offered, and provided some form of risk insurance was available.

A fundamental case for using and manipulating market forces, rather than supplanting them by direct control, is that the majority of developing countries are not control economies in the Russian sense of the term, but mixed economies where rapid growth primarily depends on the private sector. The agricultural sector comprises millions of individual decision-making units where central direction would be impossible. Similarly the manufacturing and service sectors are mostly in private hands. The failure of development plans has been fundamentally the failure of the private sector to expand at a sufficient rate. They have not expanded at the required rate often because the government has failed to provide the correct incentives and conditions favourable to expansion; the incentives have frequently gone to the wrong people.

1 But note that there is no economy in the world whose factor and product markets are not fairly well riddled with vested interests.

6.7 Conclusions

The majority of developing countries are small economies in which comprehensive planning is irrelevant. The feasible rate of growth will be determined by the 'leading' sector of the economy and thus usually depends on the possibilities for raising the rate of growth of agricultural output, and in particular raising the growth of agricultural exports. This will be achieved by using planning personnel to make detailed studies of commodity markets, for example of the possibilities for selling produce to the centrally planned economies. Secondly, the implications of these studies on the demand for resources will not require elaborate statistical exercises, because the most important linkages will be obvious to anyone familiar with the economy. At the same time, local planning and project evaluation should be undertaken so as to assist the direction of the commodity market studies. Thus, in the majority of developing countries, planning will consist of selecting leading sectors in the economy, formulating projects within these sectors and indicating the general order of magnitude of the impact of this programme on the other sectors of the economy. In this way the plan indicates the direction in which the economy should move and provides basic information on the implications of this pattern of development. This information will suggest to private entrepreneurs opportunities for profitable investment, and to the government policies which should be pursued to induce this allocation of resources.

Planning in this way will greatly increase knowledge of the operation of the economy so that, as the economy becomes more complex and the need for more comprehensive planning becomes apparent, so will the basic information for the planning be available.

This form of planning which concentrates on key sectors and the removal of important bottlenecks, may not be entirely appropriate to more complex economies such as Argentina, Brazil, India and Pakistan. However, the emphasis on devoting more attention to detailed sectoral planning is still correct.

In conclusion, Lewis (1969) has observed that planning and policy must go together, but what matters most of all is the correct choice of policies, for if the policies are right production will increase.

references and further reading

H B Chenery and M Bruno — 'Development alternatives in an open economy: the case of Israel' *Economic Journal* 1962

W A Lewis — *Development Planning* London: Allen and Unwin 1966

W A Lewis — *Some aspects of economic development* Ghana Publishing Corporation 1969

H G Johnson — 'The market mechanism as an instrument of development' in *Money, trade and economic growth* London: Allen and Unwin 1962

T Scitovsky — 'Two concepts of external economies' *Journal of Political Economy* 1954

P Streeten and M Lipton — *The crisis of Indian planning* London: Oxford UP 1968

R Vernon — 'Comprehensive model building in the planning process: the case of the less developed economies' *Economic Journal* 1966

A Waterson — 'What do we know about planning' *International Development Review* December 1965

index